Anybody Can Write

Anybody Can Write

A Playful Approach

Ideas for the Aspiring Writer, the Beginner,
the Blocked Writer

Roberta Jean Bryant

NEW WORLD LIBRARY
NOVATO, CALIFORNIA

New World Library
14 Pamaron Way
Novato, California 94949

Copyright © 1999 Roberta Jean Bryant
Cover Design: Mary Ann Casler
Text Design: Tona Pearce Myers

Library of Congress Cataloging-in-Publication Data
Bryant, Roberta Jean, 1935–
Anybody can write: a playful approach : ideas for the aspiring
writer, the beginner, the blocked writer / Roberta Jean Bryant. —
Completely rev. and updated.
p.   cm.
ISBN   1-57731-056-X (alk. paper)
1. Authorship.   I. Title.
PN145.B74   1999
808'.02—dc21   98-42425
                                                   CIP

First Printing, January 1999
Printed in Canada on acid-free paper
ISBN 1-57731-056-X
Distributed by Publishers Group West

10 9 8 7 6 5 4 3 2

For Barbara Large,
who believed in me until I could believe in myself,
and to all my students,
who taught me about the process of writing

Contents

Anybody Can Write

About Magic

Aspiring writers come to my workshops wanting *magic:* an abracadabra for getting words on paper, an open sesame for storytelling, a secret formula for success in writing.

I tell them, "There is no magic."

I do know that *anybody can write,* and I know that self-acceptance, self-knowledge, and belief in oneself are necessary to begin the struggle with words on paper. And I know it takes both trust and courage to continue that struggle.

I also know that writing is personally valuable; the act of writing is both life enhancing and potentially pleasurable. Writing, as an outpouring of creativity, can heal the spirit and nurture the soul.

No one *needs* a writing workshop, or a writing teacher, or another how-to-write book. No one needs magic to begin writing. The paradox is that when you give up the illusion of magic and settle down to work, or — better yet — to play with words on paper, to write regularly, *real magic* often happens. In this book, and in my classes and workshops, I seek to help people get from where they are now to where they want to go — with their ideas, their stories, their dreams of writing. I want to help you turn wishful thinking into successful doing, to turn you on to the experience of writing, the joy of writing, the *magic* of *you* as writer.

Part One

Anybody Can Dream

Dreamers dream. Writers write.
Poems, books, and stories evolve from
ideas, imagination, and dreams;
but only action — words on paper —
make them happen.
There are stories only you can tell.
Tell them! Tell them passionately —
with as much truth, joy,
and good humor as you can.
Begin today to make
your writing dreams come true.

Chapter One

The Dream Began . . .

When I was a pigtailed eight-and-a-half-year-old, I checked out a wonderful old book from the Santa Fe, New Mexico, public library on how to make things out of paper. "All you need," it began, "is paper, scissors, and a little gumption."

I raced into the kitchen looking for my mother. I found her outdoors on the patio weeding hollyhocks. "Mommy, do we have any gumption?" I asked, thinking it must be something like glue. Laughing, she sent me to the heavy *Webster's* unabridged dictionary in the bookcase. I read:

gump·tion (gump shun), n. Informal
1. initiative; aggressiveness; resourcefulness
2. courage; spunk; guts

Gumption was something I already had; I just hadn't known I had it. That story often comes to mind when I work with someone who wants to write. I tell that story to the hesitant ones, the fearful ones, those who feel like they just can't write — for whatever reason.

All you need if you want to write is paper, a pen or pencil — or typewriter or computer — *and* a little gumption. You don't need a fancy education or super intelligence. You don't need to know how to spell, or punctuate, or improve your vocabulary in only thirty days.

All you need if you want to write is experience — experience in living and experience in writing. Life experience you already have. Writing experience comes from your own struggles to put words on paper; writing experience evolves from the willingness to start writing and keep on writing, from honesty in telling your stories, and from dedication to learning from your writing efforts.

Willingness, gumption, and maybe some encouragement to undertake the struggle — that's what it takes. If you have willingness and gumption, the encouragement will follow.

The ability to write, like gumption, is not something you have to get, but something you already have, although you may not believe it yet. Anybody *can* do it. *Anybody can write.* Whether you're a skeptic or a believer, you wouldn't be reading this book at all if you didn't hope that *anybody* might include you too. If you possess curiosity, a little gumption, and the dream of being a writer, you can allow yourself to learn and succeed at writing.

My dream of being a writer really started the day I learned to read in the first grade. Reading unlocked a whole exciting world of happiness through vicarious experience.

The joy of reading sparked the beginning of my haphazard education in the public libraries of the West. Book learning challenged and delighted me.

School learning disappointed and disillusioned me. I hated being told what to do, hated having to read dumb and boring stuff, and I especially hated having to write. My family moved a lot; I attended nine schools in twelve years. As a natural introvert, my painful shyness and oversensitivity didn't help matters any. My grades varied: some F's, a few A's. "Working below ability" felt like high praise on my report cards.

No one ever called me a good student; I always managed to avoid writing. Any decent grades resulted from being a good guesser on multiple-choice tests rather than a good student.

In retrospect, however, I realize I was a good learner, learning from my avid reading (although I seldom read what I was supposed to). Learning things about myself rather than about school subjects. Learning that I never did anything right, or at least right enough to please the teachers. Learning that I was "lazy," that I was uncreative — learning all the ways I didn't measure up.

One day, during third-grade art class, we finally got to use the tempera paints. Many cautions about the importance of neatness accompanied the big swatch of blank newsprint we each received. "You can paint whatever you like," the teacher said.

Looking at all the colors, my excitement grew. I wanted to try every one. First I daubed some red onto the paper.

Then spatters of orange, globs of purple. Splendid! A smooth glow of yellow, wispy lines of brown. Magic! Caught up in a kaleidoscope of color, in the process of creating, I didn't hear the teacher until she stood right beside me.

"What is it?" she asked.

I thought a minute; it hadn't occurred to me that it had to *be* something.

"A flower garden?" My voice wavered, seeking approval.

She grabbed the brush out of my hand, rinsed it briskly, dipped it into the green jar, and executed a bold series of strokes across the page. My page! "This is what you want to do," she said, and then she continued on to *help* the next unsuspecting student.

My stomach hurt. I looked at how she had messed up my painting by showing me what *I* wanted to do. My idea, my fun — ruined! I wanted to rip the paper off the easel, wad it up, and stomp on it. I just sighed, however, and I supposed she must be right, and I dutifully completed it — but the magic of the doing had disappeared.

At the end of the week we had to take the paintings home. My mother loved the picture, raved about it, said how remarkable it was for a child my age. I tried to explain how the teacher had *helped,* that it really wasn't my work, that the part she liked was the teacher's doing. I knew that I hadn't painted it right.

My teachers said that writing in particular needed to be done right. Writing should be organized; writers needed to be disciplined. But I'd already learned that I was lazy, that I had a bad attitude. "Stop daydreaming," they said, so I learned to hide *Arabian Nights* behind my grammar book; I learned not to get caught with contraband books in class. They said writers needed to have talent. No one ever accused me of having talent — except a talent for wasting time.

"You shouldn't read so much. You need fresh air," my mother said, shooing me outside. So, in the summertime I hauled an armload of books outdoors into the backyard tree house. In the winter I hid in my closet with a flashlight, a pillow, and a book.

"Good girls don't tell stories," they said, which meant "don't exaggerate" or "stop lying." So, I learned to be silent. And sullen. I learned very well all the things I wasn't; I learned to feel inadequate, unworthy, uncreative. I learned how to slide through high school without doing any writing to speak of.

Nevertheless, the dream of being a writer *someday* never died. I read every how-to-write book I could find, as well as biographies of authors and volumes on writing techniques. But I seldom picked up a pencil to write a word. The sight of a blank sheet of paper always intimidated me; I felt too discouraged to even try more than a sentence or two.

I started college, dropped out, and drifted into an early marriage and motherhood still daydreaming about being a writer. I remained a functional half-literate until the age of twenty-seven: speaking only when spoken to, thinking up lots of story ideas, reading omnivorously, but writing nothing — not even letters to my mother.

Finally, I signed up to take a twice-weekly adult education class called Creative Writing. I'd been out of school for ten years, had four children under the age of five, and desperately needed to get out of the house two evenings a week.

Serendipity! The teacher loved writing and loved teaching. Her excitement — her belief that each one of us could write if we wanted to — fired my imagination. My hopes began to rise. Her enthusiasm carried me past my perceived limitations. I began writing short pieces — under two pages, but I was writing. I kept taking the same class quarter after quarter. Yes, I learned some things about writing, but more importantly, I learned some things — some positive things — about myself. The subject of writing ended up being less important than the encouragement and caring of the teacher. If she had switched to teaching differential calculus, I still would have signed up for her class.

The major reason I lead workshops today, and have written this book, is to pass on to others what she gave so wholeheartedly: infectious excitement about writing and language; joy in the expression of ideas in words and the act of putting words on paper; and a belief in the value of the individual and each writer's unique experiences and in the value of the creative struggle to transform one's daydreams into stories. I also gained a profound trust in the self and a glorious sense of possibility in what could happen from playing with words on paper. In short, I realized all the pleasures and rewards of a writing life — a life in which nothing is lost, for every personal experience is grist for the mill of the writer.

Chapter Two

Anybody Can Write?

When I pick up a new book, especially a how-to book, my approach is tentative, curious. I want to get a sense of the book and the author, want to feel it out, become a little familiar with it and get acquainted before settling down to read. First I glance at the table of contents, scan the front and back covers, and page through rapidly to see if anything engages my interest. I may begin with a section in the middle. Then, when seriously ready to read, I go back to the beginning. And if the book engages me, I read it all the way through.

How-to books often have exercises — things to do that must be done in sequence before you may turn the page. These do-not-read-further injunctions always frustrate me. Sometimes I read on anyway, and then feel as if I'm failing again to do it right. Often I stop reading altogether and mark my place, with good intentions to do the exercise (especially if it sounds interesting) before continuing. Sometimes it takes me quite a while to get back to the book.

Books offend me when they offer good ideas and information but don't give me credit for knowing how best to use them for myself. Therefore, I trust that you know how to use this book for yourself, or that you will be able to figure it out.

There's no wrong way to use this book — and there's no right way to use it either. I'd be delighted if you found it so engaging, so interesting, that you read it straight through and did all the suggested Wordplay and writing exercises as you encountered them. I'd be even more delighted if in the process of doing that you got turned on to writing and on to yourself as a person who writes.

On the other hand, maybe you're rebellious like me — more inclined to open the book up to a chapter you're curious about right now. No problem; one starting point is just as good as another. Do the writing parts when you're good and ready. Or never at all, if that's what suits you.

As a rebel I don't like following directions. School teachers and all the other grown-ups from my past told me that was bad. For a long time I believed them. Now I believe that a distrust of arbitrary, this-is-the-only-way-to-do-it directions can be a sign of creativity in action. Trust your intuition about what's good for you. Trust your creativity.

In my workshops, when it's time to write, I'll say, "Do this now. I'll be watching." I make the request and set aside class time for writing. The group agrees to play along, thereby supporting each other in following my directions.

All I can do in this book is to suggest and encourage, in hopes that you will be intrigued enough and challenged enough to try the suggestions for yourself. To try one . . . and another . . . and then, another. The writing ideas presented here are simple and very easy to do. Their simplicity is deceptive, however. They work best if you're willing to have fun with them, to approach them with a playful spirit. If you do them just for fun, you'll be more likely to have a deeper experience with them. No matter how sophisticated or educated you are, these ideas will have value for you only if you actually do them. If you're not quite ready yet to try writing, perhaps this book will help you to be ready soon, ready to be someone who can write.

The title for this book came from a student who took one of my Beginning Writing workshops. At the end of the six-hour day she raised her hand; her face glowed with accomplishment. "When I came in here this morning," she said, "I didn't believe I could write. But somehow you convinced me I can. Look." She held up her spiral notebook with dozens of hand-scrawled pages. "You know what you should call this class?" she asked. "Anybody can write," she said, *"anybody can write."* Well, I know a good title when I hear one, and I've been using it ever since.

In my workshops, there's a spontaneity in the structure. As I get acquainted with the particular needs of each group of students, my focus shifts to meet those needs. I bring along a book bag of materials — notes, ideas for writing exercises, quotes, books — but I use my experiences and those of former students as my primary resource.

This book is intended to function as a self-guided workshop for you. I wish I could see you — sit and talk with you face-to-face. I wish I could hear what you have to say, and respond to your questions, your enthusiasms, your uncertainties about writing. I'd like to be able to see when I was boring you, or making things too difficult; I'd like to know when I was explaining too much or not enough. To see you gazing out the window, or starting to daydream. To watch your foot swinging, or hear the pencil tapping or paper shuffling.

I want to share my lifelong love affair with words on paper. To share my love of books, the look and the smell and the feel of them. To share my love of writing itself, of the pen in my hand and the raggedy sprawl of the words across the smooth face of the paper. I also want to share my fascination with people who desire to write, and the difficulties they encounter in their efforts. I'd like to share my satisfaction as they get absorbed in the process of exploring and expressing their many selves through writing stories and poems and books.

Writing is a way to use everything that has ever happened in a positive and creative way. Whether you want to write because you have ideas for stories, or you want to write for your family, or you want to get published in magazines or books, it all starts with putting words on paper. In the beginning, there needs to be a lot of words.

In the last twenty years, I've worked with thousands of writers or would-be writers. My students are people like myself who never totally gave up the hope or the dream of being a writer. Some are also people like me who never did well in school, or who may feel uneducated or even incapable of being educated. Paradoxically, many of my students are multidegreed professionals afflicted with perfectionism who feel stifled by all the rules they learned to get those degrees. Both groups complain that they lack creativity, talent, or originality. They compare their efforts with those of talented friends, or measure themselves against great writers, and judge themselves inadequate. Although individual goals for writing vary widely, the common denominator in both groups is the dream of being a writer.

Dreaming of being a writer, however, is not writing. Thinking about writing is not writing. Getting excited by ideas for stories, plotting out a book in your head, reading about writing — none of these is writing.

The first law of writing is:
"To write" is an active verb. Thinking is not writing.
Writing is putting words on paper.

First one sentence and then another, or even just one word and then another. What often happens is that people try but get discouraged before they've barely started. People need to gather up their gumption, dig deep for a bit of courage. Courage is needed to begin, and to keep going.

Before you begin writing, it may be helpful to look at what the writing process is all about — to understand what happens physically, mentally, and emotionally when you sit down to write. The role that education plays in the writing process is a good place to start.

Chapter Three

Education, Einstein, and Creativity

As children, our involvement with books and reading and television and the Internet opens up a whole new world — the outer world. It's a place to learn about other people, and in learning about others, we begin to understand more about ourselves. Similarly, the world of writing affords a different perspective — that of the inner world, where learning about ourselves gives us knowledge about others. That knowledge gives us compassion and power as writers.

Children start out both curious and highly creative. We explore, touching everything we can get our hands on. We ask *why?* about everything. We don't know how things should be done, so we try it one way, then another, learning as we go — until some well-meaning parent or teacher interferes.

Creative people, of whatever age, have certain things in common. They challenge assumptions; they recognize patterns and see in new ways; they make connections and construct networks. They take advantage of chance; nothing is wasted. Mistakes are not discarded, but used as part of the solution. Most important of all, creative people take risks.

They dare to say, "So what if it hasn't been done before?" or "Maybe it hasn't been done that way before, but let's see what happens" or "Who's to say it can't be done? Let's try it out for ourselves."

This creative approach to life and learning is often stifled and ultimately destroyed by traditional education. Tradition is based on precedent: this is the way we do it because this is the way it has always been done. Public education, according to Alvin Toffler in *The Third Wave*, was an outgrowth of the industrial revolution, of the need to produce good, well-conditioned factory workers.

Therefore, besides the overt curriculum of the three R's — reading, writing, and arithmetic — there was, Toffler contends, a subtle and pervasive "covert curriculum of punctuality, obedience, and rote-repetitive work." Those learning experiences that prepared people to be good factory workers also discouraged innovation, spontaneity, creativity, and independent thinking. Creativity was not only discouraged, but also punished.

Albert Einstein recalled his relief at ending his formal education:

> It is, in fact, nothing short of a miracle that the modern methods of instruction have not yet entirely strangled the holy curiosity of inquiry, for this delicate little plant, aside from stimulation, stands most in need of freedom; without this it goes to wreck

and ruin without fail. It is a very grave mistake to think that the enjoyment of seeing and searching can be promoted by means of coercion and a sense of duty.

When higher education results in rule-oriented rigidity, the primary goal becomes not-to-be-wrong. *The fear of being wrong is the prime inhibitor of the creative process.* Ninety percent of all so-called writer's blocks come from a fear of self-exposure, *and* most people instinctively know that all writing is a form of self-exposure. Even well-defended academic writing exposes that the author is well-defended and academic.

Novelist Jessamyn West says, "To be a writer, you have to first stick your neck out and take a chance and then be willing to make a fool of yourself and give yourself away." That overwhelming sense of risk is what holds most of us back from following our wild ideas to see where they might lead.

Anaïs Nin, noted diarist, wrote: "To write means to give all. No withholding is possible. The best writers are those who give all. To hold back is an activity which withers, inhibits, and ultimately kills the seeds. The writer is exposing himself in any form, but it is a risk we must take."

Psychologist Ronald Fieve claims that creative people are usually more vulnerable emotionally; creative persons seem to lack adequate means to protect themselves, not only from the outside world, but also from themselves. "Creativity,"

Fieve says, can be "simply a response to emotional pain. Creativity is a delicate balance easily disturbed. The challenge is to encourage creativity and maintain that delicate equilibrium of optimum efficiency, so that the artist can remain extraordinarily open to new things."

Pearl Buck, novelist and Nobel Prize recipient, understood the source of creativity. She said:

> The truly creative mind in any field is no more than this: a human creature born abnormally, inhumanly sensitive. To him a touch is a blow, a sound is a noise, a misfortune is a tragedy, a joy is an ecstasy, a friend is a lover, a lover is a god, and failure is death. Add to this cruelly delicate organism the overpowering necessity to create, create, create — so that without the creating of music or poetry or books or buildings or something of meaning, his very breath is cut off from him. He must create, must pour out creation. By some strange, unknown, inward urgency, he is not really alive unless he is creating.

Chapter Four

Letting Go of Old Notions

Writing skill, creativity of expression, and even the development of talent, I ultimately found out, come not from formal education, but from one's own struggles with words on paper. From pouring out creation, as Pearl Buck said.

We're often unable to engage in that struggle, however, until we let go of some old notions and early learnings. Not only letting go of the rules of grammar, spelling, and punctuation, but also letting go of things we've assimilated from our reading, from peers and grown-ups, and from assumptions provided by our own critical faculties. We need to examine our assumptions about good writing versus bad writing.

In addition, we need to let go of things we've learned about ourselves, especially about expressing ourselves. About whether we think we're creative or talented, what we think we can or can't do, who we think we are or are not. About politeness versus honesty, and about our intelligence, our personality, our achievements.

Whether or not we've ever thought of ourselves as good students, we certainly have been good learners.

My first task in the workshops I lead is to help people unhook and detach from all the conventional education they've had. Once they've begun to do that, the education of the writer begins. Often it begins with a challenge. I make a controversial statement, such as "Thinking isn't useful in the first stage of writing."

A hand goes up. "I don't understand what you mean," someone says. Or, "How can that be true?" Those students always question; they make waves; they don't necessarily follow my advice. They are not dutiful students, but they do want to learn and often will try things out just to prove the truth of the matter to themselves one way or the other.

The students I appreciate the most are the ones who tend to be skeptical — the ones who demand value. Once these students understand that all there is to writing is *doing it,* they are ready to engage in the trial-and-error-and-error-and-error process of writing. They are also often willing to begin to trust themselves and their own experience.

I am convinced that every one of us knows best not only what to write, but also how to accomplish the task. Sometimes I give assignments or suggestions for writing exercises just to get students started. But I like it better when students use their time in class to write something they feel strongly about. To trust themselves enough not only to write it, but also to possibly share it with the class later.

As a student back in my first writing class, I had no trust in myself, my creativity, or my early attempts at writing. I'd drive home from class revved up, stimulated by everything I'd heard. Ideas bloomed grand and glorious in my head. I couldn't wait to sit down and begin writing. I'd start to write, wrestling with my idea; I'd keep at it doggedly, become frustrated, and stop. Then I'd work at it some more, struggling to improve it. I'd read it over; it was terrible, horrible, stupid! What had happened to my exciting ideas?

They were dead! Somewhere between the excitement in my head and the words on paper the ideas had died an unnatural death; somehow I'd managed to kill them off. Reluctantly, I'd drag their lifeless bodies to class, and I'd cringe in the corner when they were read aloud. The sounds of rustling papers and faint snoring confirmed my negative self-assessment. Disappointed, disillusioned, discouraged, I remembered that I wasn't talented or creative. What did I have to write about anyway? I wasn't interesting, and neither was my life. What happened with me on paper was equally dull and boring. Everyone else in class did better than I did. Dreaming of being a writer all those years had felt exciting and romantic. My reality felt awful.

I had started out thinking I had two things going for me, both due to avid reading habits: (1) a large and rich vocabulary — thanks to all the magnificent multisyllabled words I'd encountered, and (2) the many good writing techniques I'd gleaned from how-to-write books. Unfortunately,

I'd been wrong on both counts. My greatest liabilities, and the first things I had to let go of, were my overpowered vocabulary and my know-it-all attitude about technique. Only after painfully letting go of what I thought I knew about how to write well, only after giving up the temptation to show off my storehouse of inappropriate twenty-dollar words, did my writing begin to improve and come alive.

The teacher never gave up on me; she encouraged me to continue. So, despite the agony of my weekly struggle with words on paper, despite the inadequacy of my early efforts, I persevered. I kept writing because the teacher was convinced that I could improve if I worked at it. I persevered primarily, however, because shyness restricted me verbally and, by the age of twenty-seven, I had a dire need to communicate. Writing, as difficult as it was for me in those days, was still easier than talking to people over the age of five.

Within two years I'd completed a few short humor articles and sold them to my local newspaper. Humor had been the only way I could deal with the truth of my life. I'd been appalled when the teacher said, "Write what you know." I didn't like what I knew; why would I want to write about it? Ultimately, I did write what I knew as humor — employing exaggeration and an ironic tone. Of course, I began many more pieces than I completed. Writing still was painful labor for me, but I was beginning to see the value of writing for self-discovery as well as for possible publication.

One thing that kept me going was the reward of reaching an audience. My first fan letter began, "Horsefeathers!" and was unsigned. I was delighted; I didn't care that the reader thought I was an idiot. I already knew my work needed lots of improvement. My delight sprang from the fact that not only had it been published, but that someone had read it and *reacted.*

Your reaction to what you've read so far is important. Do you have a sense that some of the things you learned about yourself growing up, or negative school experiences with writing, might be blocking your dreams of writing?

The ideas presented here offer you a chance to start fresh, to begin putting words on paper, and to improve your relationship with the act of writing. You can learn to enjoy the process of expressing yourself by playing with words on paper. Let's start by getting rid of some old notions first.

WORDPLAY #1

Rapidly spill out onto paper a raggedy list of the negative notions and ideas you've learned about writing. Add any discouraging experiences you've had with writing up to this point. Don't stop to think too much as you jot down some of your bad habits and self-defeating behaviors. This list doesn't have to be exhaustive or organized in any way — take just five or so minutes to do it. (At this point, you may prefer to only think about it, or just read on through.)

Examples might include:
can't spell worth a damn
Dad says I'm too lazy
grammar's always a problem
I hate typing and my handwriting is terrible
not creative enough
writing is too much like work
I got D's in English
my cousin is a reporter and smarter than me
if I can't do it perfectly — what's the use?
I think too fast — can't slow my head down
I start things and never finish them
writing reminds me of school
can't ever do anything right anyway
I never like anything I write
procrastination is my big problem

This list will give you a sense of what to aim for. Don't spend too much time on it. Just scrawl a few notes, then put the list aside for a moment. I want to tell you a story.

In Santa Fe every Labor Day weekend, there's a big three-day fiesta. My childhood memories of the event include the carnival spirit around the plaza, the smell of roasting corn and green chiles, the brassy rhythms of mariachi music, parades and dancing and drunken brawls, and the religious candlelight procession. What I really looked forward to, however, was the finale of the celebration — the burning of Zozobra or "Old Man Gloom."

Zozobra caught my imagination and has held it all these years. A grotesque figure in a long white gown, maybe thirty or forty feet tall, Zozobra is constructed of wire and sticks like a giant marionette and his painted face grins horribly down at the gathering crowd. Fiesta goers drift toward the municipal baseball field at dusk to witness the burning of Old Man Gloom. Great groans and shrieks over the loudspeaker intensify as smoke and flames leap and curl around the effigy. Zozobra writhes and twists, and finally dies as the fireworks display begins. Cleansed and purged of gloomy thoughts and deeds, the crowd dances as star bursts of crimson and amber rain down upon them.

Southwesterners believe Zozobra personifies all their unhappiness and wrongs of the preceding year. Therefore, all the gloomy stuff, all their sorrows and difficulties, symbolically die with the end of summer. Every fall, a fresh slate — a new beginning.

WORDPLAY #2

1. Take a new sheet of paper. Using the items on the list you just made, construct or sketch with your words and phrases a stick figure, an Old Man Gloom to represent your past bad feelings about or negative experiences with writing. Here's an example:

2. After you finish filling in the stick figure with your own words or phrases, you can then throw it into the fireplace fire, or tear it into small pieces and burn it in an ashtray. Make a paper airplane out of it and sail it off a cliff into the ocean. Maybe you can think up a better way to release all of your other old notions about writing.

Now you have a fresh slate — a new beginning.

Chapter Five

Doing vs. Dreaming

Active writing is one state of being; passive dreaming about getting published is quite another. If you can learn to differentiate between the active and passive modes for yourself, you are more likely to accomplish your writing dreams and goals.

Sylvia Ashton-Warner, New Zealand novelist, writes eloquently of the passivity that plagued her ambitions:

> I've not touched my book over these three weeks. All I can show is a set of boring conclusions, glimpses, and resolutions that infest the mind like weeds when the real plant is not doing well. All this writing what I'm going to do, in living as well as working, the time alone that is squandered, the time I spend in the entrancing world of fantasy, fattening my soul on the stolen prizes of what I want to happen. Unless I economize on my daydreaming and put the savings into my thinking, what I want to happen will not happen. I must diet my soul to slim my mind. All these re-dedications, re-beginnings,

re-springings into growth of the unkillable impulse within me . . . impressive, but not a book.

Let's look at the time and energy that goes into writing, or dreaming of being a writer. What are some of the tasks that require energy? What sorts of things use up time? Here are some that occur to me:

Thinking up ideas. Jotting ideas on the backs of old envelopes. Reading books — including books on writing. Making lists of subjects for magazine articles, scenes for stories, or titles for books — to write *someday.* Taking writing classes and workshops. Beginning notes for a novel. Writing in a personal journal. Talking about writing. Going to a writers conference and listening to experts discuss writing and getting published. Shopping for just the right pen and notebook.

Dreaming up stories in my head. Wishing I had more time to write. Thinking about improving my writing. Writing letters. Organizing the papers on my desk. Researching. Sharpening my pencil. Doing the word processing tutorial on my personal computer. Writing something every day. Rewriting and more rewriting. Looking up facts in the almanac; browsing through *Bartlett's Quotations.* Creating analogies. Interviewing experts. Phoning the quick-information desk at the public library. Writing memos at work. Writing papers for school. Writing verse, or poems. Typing a manuscript.

WORDPLAY #3

1. Now, take a sheet of paper and construct your own list of time and energy activities. Use items from my list, or add some new ones — specific to your experience. You may find some of the ones I've listed don't apply to you at all.

Learn to differentiate between the productive writing you accomplish (words on paper) and the time you spend in wishing, thinking, dreaming. The next part of this Wordplay will show you how to use your list of writing activities to figure out how you're spending your time and energy in relationship to writing.

2. Take another sheet of paper and section it off into four parts as in the following illustration.

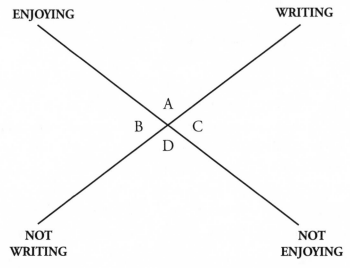

ENJOYING   WRITING

A
B   C
D

NOT   NOT
WRITING   ENJOYING

3. You'll notice that there are four categories sectioned off. Here are the guidelines for filling in each section.

In section A, *Enjoying Writing,* pencil in those activities or actions where you experience joy, delight, or satisfaction in *doing* something. The emphasis is on tangible accomplishment. "Making a list," for instance, might go here; thinking about making a list might go in section B.

In section B, *Enjoying — Not Writing,* pencil in those items that involve thinking, dreaming, fantasizing, or mental goal-setting rather than actually *doing* anything that you might be able to *show* to someone.

In section C, *Writing — Not Enjoying,* pencil in those actions where the quality of the *doing* feels like drudgery, duty, compulsion. "I have to write to my mother every week, but I don't have to like it."

In section D, *Not Writing — Not Enjoying,* pencil in those negative time wasters that you feel depressed or guilty about. "I should be writing my story, but I'm procrastinating again, and I feel bad about it."

Take five to fifteen minutes to fill out the four sections with items from your list. Some of your items may seem to belong in more than one section. If so, see if you can figure out how to break them down into smaller parts. For example, I may enjoy taking writing classes, but hate doing assignments. I may enjoy reading books on writing, but feel guilty that I'm not using the time to write. Then, list each part in the appropriate category. "Hate doing assignments," gets added to section C, but only if you *do* the assignment. Otherwise, it goes in section D.

After you're through filling in the sections, look to see how you're spending your writing-oriented time and energy. Is passive involvement such as daydreaming, nonproductive thinking, procrastination, or feeling guilty absorbing the time and energy better spent in writing?

During my first ten years of trying to be a writer I spent twice as much time and energy in mind-numbing passivity as I did in productive work with my notebook or typewriter. I agonized about my inability to write better, or faster, or more creatively rather than encouraging myself to keep writing steadily to accumulate pages — no matter how inadequate those pages turned out to be. I failed to recognize that the first task for the writer who seeks to publish is self-knowledge, and one way to get to know yourself is through writing — any kind of writing.

Ultimately, I found that for me it was better to slog through the trenches of section C, *Writing — Not Enjoying*, than to wade in section B's passive streams of thought. I've always been able to sit and think for hours and hours and have a wonderful time doing so, but I'm better off making myself sit down and crank out the pages. At least then I'll have something to show for it. New Zealand author Janet Frame confessed, "In my struggle to get my writing done I realized the obvious fact that the only certainty about writing and trying to be a writer is that it has to be done, not dreamed of or planned and never written, or talked about, but simply written: it's a dreary awful fact that writing is like any other work."

The writer's goal, of course, is to move more time and energy from passive pursuits to more active ones. For me, that meant making friends with my typewriter at first, then my computer; not thinking out or talking out my stories before setting them down on paper; either finishing what I started or not wasting time feeling guilty over unfinished work. I learned to withhold judgment until my first raggedy draft was spilled out onto paper from beginning to end. I learned to trust that my writing would spontaneously improve if I just covered a lot more pages with words.

Writer Ray Bradbury claims that ". . . quantity produces quality. Only if you do a lot will you ever be any good. If you do very little, you'll never have quality of idea or quality of output. The excitement and creativity comes from a whole lot of doing — hoping you'll be suddenly struck by lightning."

Of course, I prefer to feel good about my writing, about my involvement with writing. The better I feel about it, the more likely I am to do more of it, and then I'll feel even better about being productive. Nevertheless, I cannot let my desire for feeling good seduce me into the passive enjoyment of daydreams alone. Wonderful thoughts, story ideas, and fantasies, although pleasurable, cannot take the place of tangible pages. Over the years, not surprisingly, my writing success has been in direct proportion to the amount of time I spend at my desk producing pages.

Doing or dreaming? It's up to you. What do you want to happen? What are you willing to *do* to turn your dreams of writing into reality? What do you want to experience?

EXPERIENCE IS THE REAL TEACHER

Experience is the real teacher —
Experience in writing — and experience
in living.
Life experiences you already have.
Writing experience comes from surrender,
abandoning yourself to inspiration,
scribbling away fast and furious
like a lightning rod in a brainstorm;
fingerpainting with words,
dancing with ideas,
courting serendipity, until —
an idea comes alive and collides
with your unique spirit.
Your brainchild struggles into being then —
walks away under its own power
without a backward glance
taking your breath away.
"Wait for me," you cry, "We have work to do."

Part Two

Anybody Can Write

"The best way to learn the possibilities
is through play-exercise. Have patience!
All this play will save you many
problems later on,
and will lead you where you want
to go more quickly
than you realize."

— Gerhard Gollwitzer
Express Yourself in Drawing

Chapter Six

Beliefs, Myths, Illusions

"I don't have writer's block. Writing is just something I can't do; I've never been good with words." I often hear variations of these statements in my workshops. Many of my students really believe they simply can't write at all, or can't write well enough to justify the time or trouble involved.

These kinds of beliefs inhibit experimentation, negatively taint efforts, and limit results. Beliefs are an important source of knowledge about the world and affect the way we live and behave. Beliefs about ourselves can widen our world or restrict our experience; they can keep us from appreciating our own uniqueness as human beings, and can interfere with taking pleasure or satisfaction in what we're doing.

One of the major limiting beliefs about writing is that if you engage in writing, or have a desire to write, then you must have a definite goal; writing for publication is presumed to be the highest or most desirable goal. Writing just for fun, or for friends or family, or for yourself may seem frivolous to others by comparison. Letter writing and story-telling for children are vaguely acceptable, but certainly no match for the prestige of published writing.

Writing for self-expression or for pleasure is labeled as self-indulgent or hedonistic; such writings, critics say, have no redeeming social value. You can indulge yourself quietly as a closet writer, or engage in quasi-acceptable forms of writing such as the personal journal while in therapy, academic writing while in college, prayer diaries, business memos, or letter writing. But writing merely as a pastime or hobby has a negative connotation: it seems self-centered, and to many people a waste of time.

Even if you do want to write for a larger audience, or think you *should* because someone praised your lively letters or creative holiday greeting, the myths about *real* writers (meaning professional or serious writers) will detract from your enjoyment of writing and may not only create false standards to measure yourself by, but also false goals to aim for.

My own litany of illusions about real writers (usually meaning everybody except me) went as follows: real writers have more talent, intelligence, higher education, and degrees than I do. Real writers are more exciting, inspired, and creative than I am. Real writers love to write and do so easily (or at least more easily than I do). Real writers are free spirits, amoral, and live adventurous lives. Real writers are rich, have secretaries, and travel to exotic places. Real writers get published early, effortlessly, and often.

Confused and discouraged by this head tripping as I struggled to eke out just a few short humor articles, I found myself searching for a definition of a writer that I could live with, one that felt achievable for me. The definition I finally settled on and kept posted over my desk for years simply said: "A writer is someone who wrote this morning." I found this reminder of the daily commitment to writing helpful in getting me to my desk on a regular basis and keeping me at the task.

The French novelist Honoré de Balzac commented on the lifestyle of the writer: "We must have order in our lives so we can go crazy in our work." Eric Hoffer, self-educated longshoreman philosopher, wrote:

> They who lack talent expect things to happen without effort. They ascribe failure to a lack of education or inspiration or ability, or to misfortunes, rather than to insufficient application.
>
> At the core of every true talent there is an awareness of the difficulties inherent in any achievement, and the confidence that by persistence and patience, something worthwhile will be realized. Thus talent is a species of vigor.

So, I learned, despite my fancy and misguided notions, that real writers probably lived orderly lives and simply worked hard; successful writers probably worked harder than those who weren't successful. I learned that if I sought to write for publication I must be willing to serve an apprenticeship just as I would if I wanted to craft furniture, paint portraits, or make stained-glass windows.

Ultimately I realized that few of my ideas about real writers had any basis in reality. As it turned out, real writers struggled just like me — struggled to get the writing done, struggled to make the writing make sense, struggled to get the writing published. Writing was hard work — physically, mentally, emotionally, and spiritually demanding work — and risky at best.

Although I had always known I'd have to work harder than most people if I wanted to write successfully for publication, that knowledge was the legacy of low self-esteem rather than a true appreciation of the rigors of apprenticeship. Otherwise, I was as unprepared for most of the realities about writing as are many of my students when writing class begins.

During that first class, I now suggest that writing for publication is not the only desirable goal; writing for oneself or friends and family is worthwhile because the act of writing is life enhancing. And not-for-publication writing is much easier to do than writing that must compete in the business world of publishing.

Nevertheless, if writing for publication is your ultimate goal, it can be useful to understand your motivation. Do you want to *be a writer* or do you have stories, articles, and books that pester you to write them? Are you full of fantasies of what it would be like *to be a writer,* or are you full of stories to tell and just can't seem to get started or to bring your ideas to written completion? These are two separate

42

orientations to the goal of writing for publication. Both kinds of aspiring writers can possibly succeed, depending on persistence and determination, but the road will be easier for the writer brimming over with stories to tell, or ideas to share. Both groups must serve an apprenticeship, the duration of which is variable, but writing your first million words is a reasonable goal to shoot for.

So, there we have it — the old practice, practice, practice advice. Not original, but necessary in any worthwhile pursuit. Here's what dancer Martha Graham says about practice in the realm of dance: "I am a dancer; I believe we learn by practice. Whether it means to learn to dance by practicing dancing or to learn to live by practicing living, the principles are the same. In each, it is the performance of a dedicated set of acts, physical or intellectual, from which comes shape of achievement, a sense of one's being, a satisfaction of spirit."

Aiming for satisfaction of spirit in our writing, let's add to those first million words with the following Wordplay.

WORDPLAY #4

1. Spill out onto a fresh sheet of paper all your beliefs about writing, writers, and yourself as a writer. What would be different in your life if you were a writer? What kinds of notions interfere with your dream of being a writer? What are your if-onlys about writing? (I'd get more writing done, if only. . . .)

Write steadily without thinking and without stopping. Aim for a stream-of-consciousness flow of words onto paper. Take no more than five to ten minutes.

2. Go back over what you've just written, and circle those beliefs that are useful and draw a line through any limiting beliefs or if-onlys.

In my search for useful beliefs, I sometimes found more help from people such as Martha Graham than from books on writing. Much of my inspiration to encourage the struggle of getting words onto paper still comes from other crafts and disciplines. For instance, here's what R. D. Culler wrote about boat-building:

> Do it. That's what it's all about: any man who wants can produce a good boat. It takes some study, some practice, and, of course, experience. The experience starts coming the minute you begin and not one jot before. I sometimes hear the wail, "I have no experience."
>
> Start. Start anything and experience comes.
>
> As one of my friends says, "It's only a boat; go ahead and build it." If the first effort is a bit lumpy, so what? There will be another much less lumpy later on.

Why can't the creation of lumpy writings be a useful form of apprenticeship? Lumpy writings encourage experimentation and *doing;* they embrace the probability of imperfection. It's not that you deliberately set out to write imperfectly; it's just that you allow your efforts to be imperfect if that's the way they turn out. Anybody can write imperfect and lumpy stories. The experience starts coming the minute you begin and not one jot before.

The Zen Buddhist theory of wabi-sabi holds that there is beauty in things imperfect, impermanent, and incomplete.

Chapter Seven

Escape Writing vs. Escape Reading

E scape writing, like lumpy stories, is another lighthearted way to work on your apprenticeship. Escape writing is based on escape reading. Everybody knows that escape reading is any kind of reading done for diversion or pleasure, a temporary escape from the daily grind, a mind-relaxing pastime. Fiction, a favorite form of escape reading, allows us to vicariously enjoy lives of adventure, suspense, drama, romance, or fantasy.

Biography and autobiography offer more escape reading, as in the books about (or by) authors, political figures, Hollywood celebrities, and sports figures. Armchair travelers can enjoy John Steinbeck's *Travels with Charley* or Paul Theroux's *Riding the Iron Rooster*. Other escape readings are self-help, exercise, and how-to books, or books on cooking, gardening, and boat-building. When we escape into the illusion of "I'll diet (or exercise or build that boat or write that poem) tomorrow," reading becomes more diversion than serious instruction.

For me, reading has functioned more as a vice than a

virtue, because it has often absorbed the free time I could have used to advance my own writing. Ultimately, it came down to the question: did I want to be a reader or a writer? Passive or active?

What I'd like to propose here is that you consider becoming an escape *writer* instead of an escape reader; especially if you are an avid reader of category or genre fiction such as mystery, western, thriller, science fiction or fantasy, romance, or glitz and glamour. Category fiction has also been referred to as formula fiction, since the ingredients of each book usually are similar. If you are familiar with the category from your reading, you have also been unconsciously familiarizing yourself with the formula ingredients. Therefore, you wouldn't have to study up on how to write a mystery or western or fantasy novel before taking pen in hand to tell yourself a story — you already know the recipe.

Another way to have fun with escape writing is to write a humorous parody of a self-help book, cookbook, or computer manual; how about a made-up biography of a favorite actor, or a fantasized autobiography of a fictional character?

I propose that you write for pleasure, the pleasure of creating your own fictional world, your own adventures, your own dramas and dreams. Make up a story or entertainment — the kind of thing you'd enjoy reading — just for the fun of it.

WORDPLAY #5

1. Make a list of the reading you do, taking five to ten minutes. Who are your favorite authors? Favorite fictional characters? What forms of writing do you prefer? Magazines? Poems? Books? Novels or nonfiction? Fantastic universes? Adventures? How much time each week do you spend on this kind of reading, or in similar escapes such as watching television or surfing the Internet? What sorts of things have you been dreaming about writing?

2. From your list of favorite readings, look for a preferred category. A good candidate would be a category of book to which you devote more than two hours a week.

3. Begin now to write a story in your preferred category. Write two pages as quickly as you can *without thinking and without stopping*. Have fun with it. Do not reread it, nor mentally critique it. Just file it, and each day for the next few months add a page or two to your file folder — just for fun.

The emphasis in escape writing is always on fun — not technique, nor literature, nor with an eye on publication. It doesn't have to make sense; it should remain for your eyes only until you're finished with it in some way. This is just for your enjoyment — to entertain yourself. Psychologist Teresa Amabile warns against the creativity-killing effects of money, competition, and other rewards that persist in our culture. "People will be most creative when they feel motivated primarily by the interest, enjoyment, satisfaction, and challenge of the work itself — and not by external pressures." If you find yourself getting bogged down in seriousness about your writing, ask yourself: what would I have to do to make this more fun for me again?

Many of today's best-known authors began writing just for themselves or a group of friends. Jane Austen, for example, wrote *Pride and Prejudice* to entertain her family. Anaïs Nin's famous diaries originally were written for herself and the father from whom she was separated; they were not intended for publication. Her serious work, surreal fiction, never became popular; Nin, ultimately realizing that the diaries were her important work, began editing them for publication. Louisa May Alcott put pen to paper to exorcise a horrendous childhood. Poet Emily Dickinson wrote for herself and her salvation — to escape a circumscribed existence. She was published only after her death.

Pursuing fame and fortune through writing is a false goal, a fool's ambition. Don't burden your apprenticeship with fancy expectations or unrealistic demands of your evolving skills. Gustav Flaubert, nineteenth-century French novelist, remarked in a letter to a friend:

> To be well known is not my main business; it can only be entirely satisfying to those with a poor con-

ceit of themselves. Besides, even then does one ever know when to rest content? The utmost reknown never slakes a man's appetite and, unless he is a fool, he almost always dies uncertain of his own fame. If your work of art is good, if it is right, it will evoke its response, it will find its place, in six months' time, in six years, or when you are dead. What does it matter?

Writing for fun, writing for personal value or from necessity, provides a solid foundation of authenticity not only for an apprenticeship, but also for a writing career.

Although some of my students began writing for fun or family and ended up getting published, more of my students — the ones who started out believing they wanted to (or should) write for publication — have ended up unpublished; they are unpublished but not unsuccessful, since they did not stop writing. They found that the act of writing, the process of writing, was so satisfying for them that they couldn't quit. The personal rewards they derived from writing were more important than seeing their work in print. Humorist Peg Bracken said, "Everyone should write their own memoir to leave a personal record." Writing a memoir or family history will bring rewards of self-knowledge and satisfaction to the living of your life.

Writing can also be a form of healing. Those who write of encounters with illness or death, or loss of any kind, reach levels of acceptance and understanding that bring them comfort and peace of mind. A friend of mine began writing due to an arthritic condition in her hands; her doctor had advised her to take up knitting or typing to keep them flexible. Creating her own worlds of science fiction on the typewriter appealed to her more than knitting sweaters and afghans.

I began my first writing class determined to get published; the very idea of writing for personal reasons I considered a waste of time. It took years for me to recognize and acknowledge how much value I've derived from the prolific writings I've done that never got published. Much of it was never even rejected since it never evolved to the point of sending it out for possible publication. My collection of unpublished writings includes over fifty spiral notebooks, ranging from seventy to two hundred pages each, full of the bits and pieces of my life; story, article and book ideas; observations, perceptions, amusing incidents; mundane "to do today" lists followed by grumblings because I didn't get it all done. It's all pretty haphazard, but wonderfully rich — rich in personal value for me.

When browsing through my collection of writings, I experience both pleasure and embarrassment. The pleasure comes from the ideas and the variety; the embarrassment is over how few of the ideas were taken to completion. Nevertheless, I feel great satisfaction in having written them at all; a satisfaction divorced from good/bad or publishable/unpublishable considerations.

Anybody can derive satisfaction from writing — not just

journal writing, but writing stories and books and poems just for the fun of it. I neither advocate nor believe that anybody can (or should) write for publication. I do believe that nurturing an idea and playing around with it — giving it life on paper — is both worthwhile and potentially fulfilling. The satisfaction of creating worlds and visions and dreams that come alive is within the reach of anybody who has the desire.

Many closet writers need to look at their writing from this viewpoint. Many would-be writers need to challenge their intent. They need to admit, at least to themselves, that they really want to write for the fun of it. They also need to admit that their own pleasure or satisfaction, or that of a small circle of friends or relatives, is justification enough, and acknowledge that the act of writing as an outlet for creativity or self-expression is a fine and noble pursuit.

In my writing each day, I seek an involvement with the process of putting words on paper, a surrender to the process of developing ideas and stories reflecting themes I feel passionate about. That involvement brings me daily pleasure, often enough to keep me coming back for more; that sense of fulfillment overshadows what ultimately happens to my writings out there in the world where words on paper become books in print.

Physician and author George Sheehan wrote:

> If you are doing something you would do for nothing — then you are on your way to salvation.

And if you could drop it in a minute and forget the outcome, you are even further along. And if while you are doing it you are transported into another existence, there is no need for you to worry about the future.

Chapter Eight

The Reality of Writing

An idea sparks like an ignited match; excitement creeps like a slow-burning fuse on a skyrocket. I want to capture the moment — full of the promise of what might happen. Will it fizzle out in a tangle of dreary clichés? Or will one bright cluster of words set off and illuminate another and another and another in dizzying bursts of fresh similes and metaphors?

Unplanned connections occur when I explore an idea. I exult and revel (and sometimes wallow) in the magnificent richness of the English language. I go to excess in early drafts; I indulge myself in searching for just the right analogy or example to prove a point. At times like these, I agree with Oscar Wilde when he claimed, "Nothing succeeds like excess."

I grab paper and pen to capture the idea before it gets away; ideas are ephemeral, like spring-blooming trilliums or a dish of ice cream in the hot sun or the attention span of a two-year-old child; there's an ever-diminishing window of opportunity before a new idea wanders past. I begin to write, and if I'm lucky a sentence or two may straggle onto paper before a lot of other things start happening, things that interfere with the flow of my writing.

The critical, evaluative side of me wants to control the process of writing. That watchdog crouching on my left shoulder knows bad writing when it sees it; it scrutinizes the first sprawling sentence or two, then whispers (or shouts) in my ear: "What kind of a first sentence is that? Where's the active verb?"

The creative part of me doing the actual writing is entranced with the idea and excited by words and possibilities; it's also about five years old — curious, friendly, and excitable — with an I-can't-wait-to-tell-you-about-it kind of enthusiasm, a jumping up and down youthful impatience. Its Achilles' heel is that it really wants appreciation and approval.

When interrupted by the watchdog's criticism, the creator dutifully scratches out the offending sentence and tries again, tries to please, tries to get it right, tries very hard to get something with an active verb in it — even though it's not quite sure what a verb is.

Finally, the creative five-year-old settles on a revised first sentence and looks to the watchdog for approval. The watchdog looks at the new sentence, sighs deeply, and says something like: "Well, I suppose, if that's the best you can do. . . ." And then, the no longer excited creative part gets to eke out each further sentence under close supervision.

Where's the fun in that? The excitement, the spontaneity, the eagerness to share is gone. No wonder I avoided writing for so many years; no wonder first drafts were so painful and difficult. No wonder so many would-be writers are intimidated by the thought of writing; no wonder people get discouraged. No wonder writing is something so many of us think we just can't do. One external factor that squelches creativity is surveillance, whether real or imagined. When we feel we are being constantly watched and evaluated, we often freeze up; we may finish our work, but perform only adequately. Some perfectionists, under the whip of their own stern self-appraisal, keep procrastinating and never get on with the job.

This stifling of our natural creativity can be blamed on old methods of traditional education. From the time we start school (or sometimes even before), when we are first given paper and pencil or crayon, we are admonished: "Think before you write. Neatness and accuracy count. Do it right if you want a decent grade." The computer revolution has exacerbated the problem, because now it's too easy to stop and go back immediately to correct a mistake. Once you stop moving forward, you begin to lose the creative flow.

We are taught to engage the rational, thinking, logical part of ourselves the minute we pick up a pen and face a blank piece of paper. Gradually, this response becomes automatic; paper plus pen (or computer) equals "think first." In high-school English classes, I was told to outline my themes, to plan ahead what I intended to say. So I'd sit and think about it for hours and get little, if anything, done. I was very good at thinking. A few times I just wrote the theme first; then, it was much easier to do the outline. But I knew I had done it backward. Wrong again.

Those who don't get totally discouraged by this sterile, no fun approach to writing learn to be logical and safe and correct at all costs. And the costs are high. Not only is the process (and often the product) dull and boring, but it also reeks with falsity. Telling the truth is not a safe thing to do; what if someone gets offended? We learn to write to meet arbitrary expectations rather than being given permission to explore our own excitements and experiences — our own truths — in our writing.

Writing is a two-stage process. The first stage or first draft of any writing project needs to be a creative stage, a time to be playful, to discover and explore ideas, to finger-paint with words. Writing too carefully and safely limits possibilities and stifles creativity. A first draft needs to be allowed to sprawl onto paper beginning to end before second-stage rewriting occurs.

Journalist and author Shana Alexander understood that when she suggested that reading "murders" writing:

> The murderer of writing is reading. The death of writing is reading. Reading back over what you have just written and realizing you could make it better

and halting your forward motion down the page in order to go back and try to improve on the first part rather than marching resolutely raggedly bravely onward down to the bottom of that page and up to the top of the next one without letup until, however imperfectly, you have stuttered out whatever you may have thought you had to say.

Try to understand the split between the part of you that wants control, the critical part that wants to do it *right* — the part that has gone to school and learned to pretend to be grown-up — and your playful child part that just wants to share excitement and likes the feel of playing with ideas and words on paper.

Then, when you get ready to write, take your watchdog part firmly by the scruff of its neck and lock it in a closet (metaphorically speaking). Do not throw away the key; your watchdog/critic will play a useful role later on during the second stage of writing — the rewriting, rewriting, rewriting stage.

Once the watchdog is safely locked away, the excited child, the creative part of you, can start playing. It scribbles down a first sentence. And then a second. Nobody is watching; no critic is making impossible demands. It keeps going, keeps playing with the colorful bits and pieces, the possibilities of the idea, following all the interesting connections and sidetracks.

A poster hanging on my office wall asserts: A creative

mind is rarely tidy. The first-stage process of wordplay is often messy at best, very chaotic, rarely tidy. It lacks precision of language, tending toward primitive expression; it indulges in bad puns and wild mixed metaphors. It doesn't know about paragraphs, punctuation, or logical progression of thought, and it couldn't care less. Expressing creativity, aliveness, and truth is what it's all about; that's all it wants to do.

The can't-sit-still youthful creator, once it gets started with nobody to inhibit it, can become happily absorbed in writing — sometimes for hours at a stretch. This creature of feelings and sensations loses track of time; it experiences pleasure in the doing. After a while it runs out of steam, leaving behind a mess of paper covered with words. At that point, it can unlock the closet and call the watchdog/critic in for a consultation. "Look," the creator says, "What do you think? What do I do next?"

This second stage, in which rewriting occurs, *needs to be deferred as long as it takes to come to some kind of a conclusion or end of the story.* Once released from the closet, the watchdog/critic, who is very good at thinking, looks at the first sentence and says, "What kind of a first sentence is that? Where's the active verb?" *The exact same comment as before.* But now there are lots of pages to critique and the critic has its chance to play a more useful role than before.

The critic scans down the first page or two and, somewhere among those first few paragraphs or pages, it finds something close to what it's looking for. It says, "Here is where this story really begins. Maybe these early pages can be moved closer to the end." Or, "I think I understand what you're trying to express here, but a specific example might work better."

Then, it can continue to offer concrete directions for rewriting, for taking the anecdotes or scenes and rearranging them into a logical and persuasive whole. That's when the writing/rewriting process becomes a collaboration between the creative heart (first-stage writing) and the critical mind (second-stage rewriting). This collaboration is totally harmonious and useful; the finished piece has the emotional spontaneity and integrity of the child as well as the orderliness the adult reader expects from written work.

Science fiction author Ray Bradbury talks about first-stage writing. "The only good writing is intuitive writing," he says. "It would be a big *bore* if you knew where it was going. It has to be exciting, instantaneous and it has to be a surprise. Then it all comes blurting out and it's beautiful. I just act and react and emotionalize and all good stuff comes out."

The second law of writing is:
Write passionately. Everybody has loves and hates;
even quiet people lead passionate lives.
Creativity follows passion.

If your first draft isn't driven by passion, if it doesn't come alive with good stuff, if it doesn't crackle with excitement, your second draft will be jeopardized by a shaky foundation.

Many important considerations can be tackled during rewriting; blending in emotional authenticity is not one of them. Therefore, what you want to capture in your first writing is that emotional aliveness, that excitement, that crackle.

Chapter Nine

Getting Hooked on Writing

Sunday morning — a writing day for me. I'm wearing navy sweat pants, a turquoise jacket, my lucky purple socks, and pink and gray jogging shoes. I just returned from forty minutes of roving (a combination of brisk walking and easy jogging). I'm no athlete, but I get out in the fresh air every writing day to stimulate the creative flow. The rhythmic movements and deeper breathing pull oxygen into my brain, loosen up my body, and dust away the mental cobwebs.

As I jogged past two churches, I saw people all dressed up coming from or going to religious services, and it occurred to me that my writing days, my writing time, had become sacred for me. My ritual includes roving in the fresh air, a giant cup of coffee, a quiet working space, and the preliminary five-minute writing warm-up in my journal, all of which help bring me as fresh and as empty as possible to my desk.

At my desk, I take dictation from my playful, inquisitive, five-year-old self, making myself available to tap into a kind of collective creativity. And I religiously set aside and protect my time for writing, showing up each writing day to see what will happen, allowing for all sorts of possibilities. I also wrestle with the demons of self-doubt, each day performing an act of faith that a certain story, or book, or train of thought might, in the long run, turn out to have been worth telling, to have been worth the time, the energy, the hard labor.

I study creative principles, my own creative process, my habits and motives, to learn enough about myself to discover what works and what doesn't work for me. I continue to make mistakes — learning from the time-honored trial-and-error method. I show up. "Ninety percent of life is showing up," says filmmaker Woody Allen. I set to work despite my fears. "Ninety percent of talent," said actor Fred Gwynne, "is lack of fear."

My daily roving in Lincoln Park functions not only to stimulate the creative flow, but also provides a perfect analogy for my writing process. If I've not run for a while, my body feels draggy as I begin the course. It's difficult to keep going for a whole minute at a slow jog — even downhill to the beach. My muscles tire quickly. Aches and pains surface. I just can't do this any more, I think.

I encourage myself to keep going anyway. The first ten to fifteen minutes alongside Puget Sound are the hardest. Sometimes I slow to a walk or pause to catch my breath, but I press on. Keep going, I tell myself. Keep going, keep going, keep going.

Then comes Heartbreak Hill, a steep trail of switchbacks to the top of the bluff. I aim to climb it steadily with as few stops as possible. When I do pause, sweating and gasping loudly, I wonder if it's worth the effort — but I'm at the point of no return. It's as far to go back the way I came as it is to press on. So, onward and upward, I persevere. The view of Maury Island across the sound helps me regain my breath, and a second wind. I start to run, feeling limbered up; there's a sense of ease and strength and purpose. And pleasure.

I just keep on, keep on, keep on. Movement feels effortless, until the path rises again. If I keep my eyes down, looking for that next step and take each one as it comes, I tend to notice the grade much less. If I fix my gaze at the top, I see how steep it looks and tire more quickly. Sometimes I slow down and walk awhile. Finally, I'm at the top. Then comes the best part, a slight downgrade all the way back to my car. It's like flying. No stress. No strain. Just the pure joy of moving, of physical expression. I don't ever want to stop. The end of my course is in sight. I've persevered, had a good workout. I've experienced both pleasure and discouragement, but I've made it.

Each day thereafter, even if I only run three or four days a week, it usually gets easier — except for the odd day. On that day I don't even feel like getting up, much less getting dressed and going outside to run. I think I'm coming down with a cold, or something worse. But I really don't want to lose momentum, so I drive to the park and begin to move anyway.

My body is leaden; I've forgotten how to breathe; my legs work funny. My side hurts; my head aches; each step is hard labor. Following the trail to the bluff is agony; it never gets much easier, though there are a few minutes when it's less worse. And finally, relief that it's over. I survived.

The next morning I usually can't wait to get started, and the ease and pleasure are heightened. The important thing is that each day brings a different experience. Doing it anyway — especially on the difficult days — is always worth it. Once in a while, I get a string of bad days in a row. The challenge is to keep on, knowing it will eventually get easier.

Writing is exactly like that for me. Always, when beginning a new writing project, it takes a while to get into condition, to get the hang of it, to gain momentum. Some days I just go through the motions, maintaining the schedule, doing it today, doing it anyway.

I need to keep to a regular schedule at my desk, and I need to protect and guard that time against the encroachment of phone calls, domestic tasks, distractions, or interruptions. When an emergency occurs, I allow myself time out with no penalty; the extra time it takes to get back into the flow is penalty enough.

What I'm aiming for with my writing, as well as my running, is making a habit of it. It takes twenty-one days to make or break a habit, to retrain automatic responses. If I can get past the twenty-first day in my writing, or my running, I've established a familiar routine and I feel deprived if I have to miss out on the experience.

In running, there's a physiological reason for this. The running stimulates the production of natural, morphinelike secretions in the brain that stimulate feelings of pleasure and well-being. Thus, I've become addicted to either repeating the experience or suffering withdrawal symptoms. I am, in short, hooked — hooked on a self-reinforcing positive addiction that has a beneficial influence on my quality of life.

Getting hooked on writing, the habit of writing, is my challenge. With writing, there's no physiological addiction. Writing is a sedentary business, the application of the seat of the pants to the seat of the chair, the words to the page. Yet, the habit of writing can become a positive addiction, so that a missed day at my desk evokes withdrawal symptoms. The habit of writing stimulates the creative hemisphere of the brain, the source of emotions — including pleasure.

Ideas sparking plus words flowing plus pages accumulating equals satisfaction. I get hooked on the hours spent in the creative mode where time disappears and the quality of experience is more like pleasure or delight than work. A former student, who had felt blocked from writing for a long time, dropped me a note: "I'm writing again," he said. "It's better than sex."

WORDPLAY #6

The habit of flexing your writing muscles with a five-minute daily warm-up is a good one to cultivate. Even on nonwriting days, the five-minute warm-up will help you stay in practice. Anybody can write for five minutes.

The secret is to keep the pen moving on the paper the whole time; no stopping to think. If you must think, do your thinking on paper. Pretend you're a pianist playing scales; repetition is okay. Punctuation and grammar are irrelevant.

1. Take a word, phrase, or idea, and play with it. Poke at it; make fun of it. Speculate. Ruminate. Cogitate. Meditate. All on paper. Take any word. Any phrase. Any idea. Whatever. (Or choose one of the following: spaceship; if Monday is blue, what color is Friday?; mortgage; forsythia; high as a kite; mother; werewolf; travel; don't frighten the horses.) *Start now.*

2. Make a list of twenty-one words, phrases, or ideas to use in future five-minute warm-ups.

Here's one of the warm-ups I did while working on this book:

> Ideas — exciting, delightful, intoxicating. I love the sensuous feel of words tumbling onto paper — gloriously messy. Satisfying, like finger painting. The smoothness of notebook paper, of different pens gliding along its surface. I like struggling with an idea, clothing it in words, and sending it out fetchingly dressed to catch the attention of the world. I like that part of the process where it's like a big

jigsaw puzzle, rearranging and reordering the pieces to make a logical picture with the fragments. I like to share ideas, communicate with an unseen audience. It's scary and marvelous when the creative flow begins and floods. The challenge: to hang in there when I'm stuck until something moves, until something happens. Practicing what I preach about writing is humbling, sometimes humiliating, but always fulfilling. I'm happy when I'm learning. Words on paper always mean learning. Word tripping is fun — pure and simple.

Chapter Ten

The Power of Your Uniqueness

Growing up, the messages we receive from society encourage modesty of expression and reward emulating others. The result is that many of us tend to devalue or downgrade our personal experience of life and learning, as if the everyday ordinary events, and even our special ones, aren't special enough to be talked about, much less written about. And yet, that's all we have to offer, to share with others, in our writing: our inadequate selves, our opinions, our experiences, our uniqueness.

I used to envy anyone who had a normal childhood or happy school experiences. My early experiences hid out in a mental compartment labeled Miserable Childhood. Even after I started writing and getting published, I avoided writing about my upbringing; I didn't think anyone would be interested.

One day in a writers' workshop, a woman named Beth complained about the regimentation of her childhood, her lack of personal freedom in growing up. I said that I envied the attention and family closeness that had been part of that package; I mentioned my lack of supervision and my feeling that nobody really cared what I did. I told her about my peculiar on-again, off-again education, and my tomboyhood spent hiding out in tree houses.

The whole class not only listened, but also reflected fascination — and envy. "Tell us more," Beth said. Another woman suggested I write a book about it. Up to that point, it simply hadn't occurred to me that my growing up experiences might be useful material for writing. I began evaluating the things that had happened to me in a different way. I realized that I could separate usable bits and pieces — the anecdotes, conversations, and minidramas — from the unusable. I could sort through them, putting some of them in a box newly labeled Unconventional Childhood.

My mother had a button box full of buttons in all colors, sizes, and shapes. I hated sewing; my dolls were naked and neglected more often than not. But the button box, a round blue tin with a gold scroll design on top, intrigued me. I always needed buttons for those projects that consisted of paper, wood, or yarn — the projects that required gumption. I'd paw through the box, then dump the contents out on the rug, touching all the various textures, looking for buttons that matched or would suit my purpose. My fascination with the button box often sidetracked my projects. I'd sort the buttons by size, color, and shape; seldom were any two buttons alike, but some could be grouped together even though they weren't identical.

My mental storehouse of rich and varied experiences is like that button box: a place where I can find just the right touch to make a point or finish off a story. Quite a few of them, for example, popped up to be used in this book.

Nowadays, I play with the other boxes I've collected in that mental storehouse. From the box labeled Childbearing and Heir-raising comes "The PTA Dress" — about the only item in my wardrobe that made me feel grown-up enough to be a parent. From my Naive Divorcée box comes "Freelance Human Being" — my answer to being asked what I did in my search for an identity beyond marriage and motherhood, and "My Hitchhiker" — about a trip to California and my encounter with someone who felt like an older brother from the moment we met.

All useful. All valuable. All potentially interesting to other people. I've discovered that things that happened to me are relevant to people with similar backgrounds, because it validates their experience, and relevant to those with different or opposite backgrounds because it satisfies a curiosity about how the other half lives.

Unfortunately, the false modesty, politeness, and rules of behavior imposed on us by society all conspire to convince us that we — and therefore, our true feelings — are not okay. We are told to reform our bad habits, to behave appropriately, and — most important — to improve ourselves.

These influences lead us to invalidate our personal experience, and to hesitate before making independent decisions.

We look to authorities for answers, for guidelines, for permission. We check things out — first with teachers and parents, then with bosses or government bureaucrats or therapists or other so-called experts.

Sometimes the first step towards unlocking the writer within each of us is to reclaim the power and authenticity of our own experience. If you're old enough to read this to yourself, *you have all the experience you need to begin to write. If you're over forty, you have all the experience you'll ever need to write and write and write and never run out of interesting things to write about.*

I can just hear the protests at this point. "But I had an ordinary (or happy) childhood." "But I'm just a postal clerk (or student or mother or bookkeeper or waitress)." "I've never traveled out of the state I was born in." "I've never sinned or suffered or repented enough to have anything interesting to write about."

"Horsefeathers," I say. What do you like? Dislike? What do you love? Hate? What frightens you? Fascinates you? Where were you when President Kennedy (or Reagan) was shot? What did you feel when that happened? What were you doing when the Berlin wall fell? How did your family feel when the Vietnam War (or the Gulf War) ended? What world event captured your attention? Why? What personal loss has most affected you? How did it feel to fall in love (or like, or lust) for the first time? What has thrilled you? Disappointed you? Who has had a more interesting life than you? How do you feel about that? What are your dreams? Your fears? Your fantasies? Your satisfactions?

All these events are part of your experience. Your unique point of view, your thoughts and your feelings about these events are worth writing about. If that still doesn't seem like much, or enough, to set you to writing, you'll find some exercises in the next chapter that may stimulate your imagination and get you excited about writing.

If you've had difficulty trusting yourself, trusting the power of your own experience, perhaps you'll trust me for a while. Trust my years of experience helping people become writers, helping each writer find his or her own unique voice, helping people get from where they are with their writing to where they want to go.

"Trust me," I ask new students, "There's method in my madness." I assure you that *anybody can write*. What's true is that a lot of people don't even want to. But if you do want to, you can do it. All you need is the willingness to experiment with words on paper. Anybody can write — *if they want to write.*

Chapter Eleven

The Writing Experience

Up to this point, you've had the opportunity to indulge in a little Wordplay, but mostly you've been reading about writing. You've read about the possibility of writing, about the value of words on paper, about doing it easily, or at least doing it. We've talked about having fun with writing; about giving yourself permission to write just for self-discovery; and about expressing your ideas, your creativity, your uniqueness in writing.

Now it's time to experience writing. This first writing process I'll describe embodies some powerful and versatile techniques for changing your experience of writing for the better. This three-part writing process is deceptively simple. At first, it may sound childish, frivolous, or peculiar. It may be all those things, but I guarantee that if you'll try it, and especially try to get into the spirit of the exercise, you'll find it surprisingly valuable.

What you're going to be asked to do with words on paper may feel somewhat strange, unless you had a very creative third- or fourth-grade teacher. Think of this process as another warm-up, a five-finger exercise, a zero draft. A zero draft is one that doesn't count; it can be wadded up and thrown away afterward if you don't like it. A zero draft is sometimes done on the back of used paper, so there's nothing wasted if it doesn't work out.

There are only two rules:

1. *Write steadily and without stopping.*
2. *Write without thinking.*

How can you write without thinking? You just keep putting words on paper without demanding that they make sense. I used to spend all my writing time thinking, thinking about what to write, where to begin, discarding one approach after another. Thinking, thinking, thinking — and nothing happening on the page. All that thinking for zero results. *Thinking is not writing.* Writing is putting words on paper.

It may, of course, be impossible to write without thinking. Stray thoughts may come up such as, "This is really dumb and stupid," or "I don't know how to do this right," or "I wish I knew what was expected of me." If they do, write those thoughts down — in the middle of a sentence, if necessary. What I discovered about this freeflowing writing process is that there's no right way to do it. There's no wrong way either. There's just doing it or not doing it. The purpose of this exercise is to practice the act of putting words on paper; making sense of those words can come later if needed.

The other thing to remember, besides the not thinking, is: *Keep the pen moving steadily across the paper all the time.* No pausing to figure out the right word; leave a space if you need to and continue on — no stopping to wonder what to do next, no stopping the stream of consciousness flow of words onto paper. I suggest writing by hand with pen on paper for these preliminary exercises; the physical act of writing the words seems to enhance the process.

If you are a good typist, however, and prefer to use a typewriter or computer, find a way to cover up what you're doing so you won't be tempted to read it over or correct mistakes. With a computer, you can blank out the screen by turning the monitor off or draping a towel over it, or use your detachable keyboard to face away from the screen.

The don't-think-don't-stop approach seems to enable the writer to bypass the critic, to stimulate the creative flow, and have fun with writing. The secret is to feel uninhibited enough to just put anything down on paper, especially if you feel stuck or blocked. If that should happen, simply write down what's true for you about what's happening: I don't know where to go from here; I don't have anything more to say about this; I wish the time was up; I feel stuck; I feel stuck; I feel stuck.

Usually what happens when you acknowledge the obvious is that you will get bored before you can cover half a page with "I feel stuck." Then, you'll get back on track and find yourself doing something different.

WRITING EXERCISE #1
PAPER AND PEN CONVERSATION

This is a three-and-a-half-part exercise. I suggest allowing five minutes for each part; or, write two or three pages until you feel stuck — then do another half page past the point you felt stuck.

All you need is paper and pen (or pencil, or typewriter, or computer) and a little gumption. Once you begin writing, write steadily. No thinking. No stopping. No right way. No wrong way. Just doing it.

Part 1: For the next five minutes, or three pages, pretend you are the piece of paper (or the computer screen) you're writing on. Use the first person, the "I" point of view. For example: "I am the piece of recycled paper Jean chose to write on today. My life began as a piece of junk mail, advertising a water bed sale; now my other blank side gets to be useful. I'm glad to have a chance to express myself today even though it feels strange to have a voice. I can't wait to see what I have to say. . . ." You, the writer, make yourself available to record what the paper might have to say for itself, about itself, about the world. Include its hopes and dreams. Allow the piece of paper to say what it's most afraid of. Think of yourself as taking dictation.

Begin now.

Part 2: Now that you've given the paper you're using a chance to express itself, it's only fair to give equal time to the writing instrument you're using; whether pen, typewriter, or computer keyboard. For example: "I'm the ballpoint pen Jean rescued from the oblivion of her purse. I've been feeling lost and lonely down there for a long time. It feels good to be moving again and I have a lot to say. . . ." Write again for five minutes or three pages. *Have fun with it.* Don't forget to write steadily; keep the pen moving on the paper the whole time.

Part 3: Now that you've gotten these two inanimate objects talking in their own voices on paper, record a conversation between them. For example: Paper might say, "We're supposed to talk to each other, but I don't know how to begin."

Pen: "Looks like you already have. You sure didn't give me a chance to say something first."

Paper: "I can't help it if you're slower than I am."

Begin now. Five minutes or three pages. Keep going.

Postscript: Here's the last little bit, the "half" of the three-and-a-half-part exercise I referred to earlier. Now that you've gotten these inanimate objects talking, there's an opportunity to find out what words of wisdom they might have for you, the writer. Write out a question to ask them. Then record their answers. For example: "What advice do you have for me today?"

Paper: "Who needs advice when you can have fun? I hope we can do it again sometime."

Pen: "Don't forget me; this couldn't have taken place without my help."

This is an easy and playful technique for getting words on paper. If you're just beginning to acquire the habit of writing, doing this exercise for fifteen or twenty minutes a day can limber up your writing muscle, and make you more comfortable with the act of writing on a regular basis.

This technique is called projection; you instinctively project your own thoughts and feelings onto the object whose viewpoint you're exploring. Projection is something you're already skilled at even though you probably have not been consciously aware of it. Pick inanimate objects to begin with, since they do not have thoughts or feelings you can readily interpret. Projection is extremely versatile when done as a writing process; its usefulness to you will be limited only by your imagination. I encourage you to play with it.

Writer Madeleine L'Engle claims that her work as a writer *is* play: "Watch children at play," she advises. "They are terribly serious about it — even running into a jump rope. You're very serious as you get in, to be sure the rhythm is there; as you're jumping, it gets less serious and more play.

The same thing is true with writing. The first fifteen to twenty minutes, or half-hour, is getting into that rhythm. Then, once you're in it, you get caught up in the rhythm. That's when it really gets to be complete play."

WRITING EXERCISE #2
PROJECTION TECHNIQUE

Pick any object in the room, or in view, or in your mind's eye. You could choose your right tennis shoe, your car, or the teddy bear you had as a child. Make yourself available to let the object express itself on paper using the first-person point of view: "I am. . . " Think of yourself as taking dictation. After the object has told you as much as possible about itself, you can have more fun with it. Ask it questions, record its answers, enlist its help with the stories you'd like to write.

Aim to do two or three pages, or spend five minutes, or write until you feel stuck and then *do one more page.* Even if that extra page ends up as nothing but gibberish, in the long run, the willingness to *write one more page* when you feel like giving up, or think you've run out of things to say, will pay handsome dividends in earning your apprenticeship and acquiring the habit of writing.

Chapter Twelve

Anything Goes — Journal Magic

"Keep a daily journal," my first writing teacher advised. "That's the best way to get comfortable with putting words on paper." She assured me I'd gain the writing facility I lacked by starting a journal.

Great advice. The best advice about writing I've ever received, as a matter of fact. But it fell on deaf ears; I really couldn't see the point of beginning what seemed like just another tedious writing chore. I wanted desperately to write to publish, and anything less serious seemed a waste of time. After all, what could you do with a journal? My notion of a journal was a place where you wrote about your feelings, an adolescent confessional, a "Dear Diary." Who needed that? Not me.

I had heard about a writer's journal that could be used like an artist's sketchbook — a place to record story ideas, fragments of overheard conversation, descriptions of places or seasons of the year. Despite being intrigued by the idea, I resisted beginning a writer's journal for almost a year.

Summer vacation approached, and the prospect of no

classes for three months prompted me to look for a writing project to do so I wouldn't lose the momentum I'd gained during the school year. Okay, I decided, I'd try a journal, but it had to be a writer's journal. I assigned myself one page a day, one side of the page, in a wide-lined, spiral-bound note-book. And I'd do it before going to sleep at night.

I started feeling excited by the possibilities. Lyrical descriptions, article and story ideas, invented dialogues. Maybe I'd even do some poetry. Grand ideas. Good plan.

The first day came. Night fell. Bedtime approached. I took out the notebook, rounded up a pen. I thought and thought. Scribbled a few lines, feeling dumb. I struggled to describe that evening's sunset; I reread the few sentences I'd produced and judged them as lifeless and boring. I eked out the rest of the page as an act of discipline. I felt frustrated, angry, disillusioned. The final line on that first page read: "You even show off your big vocabulary to yourself!" Not an auspicious beginning with my internal critic taking a pot-shot at me.

Nevertheless, I kept my agreement to do one page a day over the summer, despite painful barbs from the critic. That one page every day was the hardest thing I'd ever done; I felt humiliated that I was producing a boring diary rather than the exciting writer's journal I'd envisioned. But I persevered, hoping the effort would ultimately be useful. By the time class resumed, the diary-journal was a useful habit, one I've benefitted from ever since. My journal not only turned out to be personally valuable, but also served as a source book for some of my published writings.

The first task of the writer who seeks to publish is a challenging one: self-knowledge. Journal writing is a great way to gain self-knowledge as well as work on your apprenticeship. A journal is one of the best vehicles for exploring your life through writing. If you can keep the critic at bay, if you can allow yourself to record the truths of your life, if you can withhold judgment, the time spent on creating a journal can pay off more than anything else I know.

Privacy is an important consideration; you must protect your journal from prying eyes, or even from casual reading by others. Avoid showing it to friends and loved ones. Any kind of exposure can be detrimental because you may start being too careful and lose truth and spontaneity in your writing. If you keep your journal on your computer, use a password to preserve privacy. If you prefer a handwritten journal, choose the type of notebook that feels comfortable for you and find a way to keep it private. Friends often give me those fancy or leather-bound blank journals with heavy unlined paper. I can't bring myself to write in them because I feel too inhibited. They seem to demand a perfection I know I can't achieve. The total permissiveness I need for journal writing works best for me with inexpensive spiral notebooks.

"I've been doing personal writings for over three years," one of my students told me. "But journal is too formal a word for what I do, and diary is too juvenile. So I call it my 'anything goes' book." What a wonderful idea, I thought. "Anything goes" imposes no limits on my imagination, no curbs for my creativity. And it covers all the uses to which I subject my spiral notebook — pasting in fortune cookie maxims, daily horoscope predictions, first drafts of love letters and angry letters — unlimited possibilities.

An anything goes type of journal is the easiest way to create a therapeutic relationship with yourself. Use your journal as a portable friend. Give it a name such as Greg or Joy or Hannah, so you can share your journal insights with others in a benign way: "As I was telling Hannah the other day. . . ."

The anything goes journal could be one way to explore all the ideas in this book and invent some playful ones of your own as well. As a matter of fact, many of these suggested writing processes are adaptations of journal techniques that I discovered were useful for facilitating any kind of writing. If you began an anything goes notebook and did nothing but variations of the Wordplay suggestions for a year, I guarantee you would be astonished and delighted with the results.

A nonthreatening, no-demands journal that is protected and private can provide the perfect place to write at risk, to say all the unsayable things, to tell things like they really are — like they really are for you. A secret place to risk being honest with yourself.

The third law of writing is:
Write honestly. Risk nakedness.
Originality equals vulnerability.

I like what Jessamyn West says about being a writer: "To be a writer, you have to first stick your neck out and take a chance and then be willing to make a fool of yourself and give yourself away." A journal provides a safe place to practice doing just that.

A journal is a place to detail all the little happinesses and document all the large delights of your unique life. A place to have fun. And a place for magic. Magic happens when one engages in regular and long-term involvement with oneself in words on paper. Journals need not be grim or boring. Expressing the joys of your life, appreciating what's good today, playing with ideas — all are potentially magical.

TRUSTING YOURSELF

Trust yourself. Trust your experience. Trust your
hunches, your opinions, your feelings.
Trust your uniqueness as a vulnerable human being
who has experienced life in a different way from any
other individual, past, present, or future. There are no
new ideas — only new perceptions,
new ways of seeing things, fresh points of view.
Trust yours.
As a writer, the only thing you have to offer the world
is your own unique self. Be courageous. When you
think, "Oh, I can't write that part; it's too petty, too
shameful. It's not respectful. People won't understand"
— ignore these subversive thoughts. Be willing to say
whatever you have to say truthfully (full truth). Trust
yourself, and trust your potential reader.
When you trust the truth, you can have the courage
to write at risk.
Trust your intuition, your absurdities, your loves,
your hates. Most of all, trust your passions,
those extra-strong feelings and urges that flow
and surge and pulse with aliveness.
Passion provides momentum, involvement,
commitment, action.
Trust passion.

Part Three

Everybody Has Difficulties

"In order to write a book, it is
necessary to sit down
(or stand up) and write.
Therein lies the difficulty."

— Edward Abbey
A Voice Crying in the Wilderness

Chapter Thirteen

Arm Wrestling Self-Doubt

"Every day when I begin to write, I face that big hairy beast," someone once remarked in class. The big hairy beast she referred to was her insecurity, her doubts about herself, the voices in her head that pursue her with questions: What makes you think you have anything to say? What's the use? It's all been written before. You can't do it well enough, so why bother?

Self-doubt assails the best of us from time to time. Prolific British novelist Anthony Trollope admitted, "There are some hours of agonizing doubt, almost of despair. . . ." Even American novelist John Steinbeck wrote, "I'm scared, but I think that is healthy. It is perfectly natural that I should have a freezing humility considering the size of the job to do and the fact that I have to do it all alone. There is no one to help me from now on. This is the writing job, the loneliest work in the world. And I am now going into the darkness of my own mind."

Thinking too much, instead of plunging in and playing with words and ideas on paper, squelches your playful energy, retards your production of pages, and limits your possibilities. Pay no attention to the gremlins of discouragement, lest you talk yourself out of writing at all, lest you lose your belief in yourself.

Be willing to experiment. As Carl Jung once wrote:

> Every one of us gladly turns away from our problems; if possible they must not be mentioned, or better still, their existence is denied. We wish to make our lives simple, certain and smooth — and for that reason problems are taboo. We choose to have certainties and no doubts — results and no experiments — without even seeing that certainties can arise only through doubt, and results through experiment.
>
> When we must deal with problems — we instinctively refuse to try the way that leads through darkness and obscurity. We wish to hear only of unequivocal results and completely forget that these results can only be brought about when we have ventured into and emerged again from the darkness. But to penetrate the darkness we must summon all the powers of enlightened thought that consciousness can offer. We must even indulge in speculations.

One secret of success in writing is to do that speculation on paper, not in your head. Overthinking results in paralysis by analysis. You wonder which idea to pursue or which point of view to use. You can't decide, so you do nothing.

Here are a couple of frivolous-sounding yet very practical ways to simplify those kinds of choices. Most people are familiar with this first one: it's called "Eeny, meeny, miney, moe." This nursery rhyme method works because if you really don't know which choice is best, it doesn't make any difference; choose any one. The second decision-making process is useful when you have only two choices: you simply flip a coin. Heads, one option; tails, the other. The secret is to *pay attention to your emotional response* to the choice that comes up; *then follow your response,* rather than what the coin indicates. Freud, himself, suggested this idea, the point being that the coin toss and your reaction to it give you some information not in your conscious awareness.

Creative excuses often absorb writing energy. One student complained that reading her favorite authors, instead of stimulating her own work, caused her to feel inferior: "Oh, I can never do as well as that." She made the mistake of comparing her zero-draft explorations with edited and polished professional work, and said, "I can't." *Can't* has the same results as *won't.* Also, I've learned to avoid reading the types of things I'm currently writing. Instead, I look for the kind of reading that inspires and renews me, but doesn't lend itself to easy comparison.

"I could try, I guess," a young man reluctantly admitted when I challenged his constant — and creative — excuses for not writing. Trying is an illusion, I told him. Writing is doing it. In between, there are only empty gestures, half-hearted movements that always stop short of completion. Trying is thinking about doing it; the minute you put pen to paper you have started doing it. "I tried" is a passive excuse. There's only writing or not writing.

Writing produces words and sentences and accumulates pages. Picking up the pen or sitting in front of the keyboard isn't enough. You must activate the tool; lend your fingers and hands and spirit and will to put the tool in motion; provide the energy to keep putting words onto the page.

"Easy for you to say," the skeptics in the class challenge. Easy to say? Of course. Easy to do? Not necessarily. It's not easy to overcome self-sabotage; it's not easy to change a lifetime of I can'ts, I won'ts, or I trieds.

"To know how to write is a great art," says historian and essayist Jacques Barzun. "Convince yourself that you are working in clay, not marble; on paper, not eternal bronze; let the first sentence be as stupid as it wishes. No one will rush out and print it as it stands. Just put it down; and then another. Your whole first paragraph or first page may have to be guillotined after your piece is finished; but there can be no second paragraph until you have a first."

The first step is to be willing to do that first paragraph anyway — any which way. Just keep the pen or fingers moving until your self-assigned writing time is up. That's all — it's as simple and as difficult as that to acquire the habit of writing and the momentum that will keep you going; to prime the wellspring of ideas, creativity, and individuality that everyone possesses; to write despite the fear of failure — or fear of success.

Fear is a form of self-doubt. Fear of not pleasing someone in your life; fear of not doing it right, not measuring up, not doing it perfectly. Perfectionism, the stepchild of fear, is one of the biggest killers of creativity. Perfectionists set unrealistic standards of production or performance for themselves; they have inflated expectations regarding time or energy or originality or the number of drafts needed. Unfortunately, many of the most perceptive, creative, and sensitive people are afflicted with perfectionism.

If the pursuit of perfection afflicts your dreams of writing, it is important to remove any performance bond from your early writings. The task is to eliminate the success/ failure trap from zero-draft, first-stage writing, and cultivate an attitude of allowing things to happen on paper. Encourage your natural spontaneity and playfulness. Encourage means "to inspire with courage, spirit, or confidence. To breathe spirit into." Courage is defined as "the quality of mind or spirit that enables one to face difficulty, danger, pain, with firmness and without fear; bravery."

So, the antidote to self-doubt is courage; perhaps just the courage to be dreadful. And if the critic in you refuses to stop judging, the courage to be dreadful might be useful. Even more useful is the realization that the critic within you has two voices, two personae. The troublemaker critic says things like: "You numbskull," or, "How could you be so stupid?" or, "That writing is really bad." This voice is destructive; all it does is make you feel bad.

The constructive critic, the one worth listening to, *always tells you something you can do;* it seldom indulges in good/bad, right/wrong judgments. This useful critic says things like: "That's not clear; why don't you try this?" or, "This could use a specific example to prove your point." The good critic always offers suggestions tentatively; it wants to help, not to control.

Challenge your internal critic to suggest, not condemn. Breathe deeply as you search for the inspiration and courage to experiment your way through the despair of your struggles with writing, the darkness and obscurity and confusion of your ideas. Writers, according to psychologist Ronald Fieve, "described experiences of being flooded with emotional stimuli which they were unwilling to block off. This flooding resulted in a confusing variety of conflicting passions, ideas, and diversions." That sort of confusion, which often feels like self-doubt, is simply one more stage that precedes clarity. If you begin feeling confused with your writing, remind yourself that beyond the current muddle lies the clarity you seek. And if no solution presents itself, write something, even if it's dreadful.

Self-doubt cannot survive that daring leap into the unknown. Sometimes I will simply copy over a few paragraphs already written, hoping that this action will start the flow, the forward movement, again. Taking action is always useful in writing. I often begin my writing by spilling out onto paper, for only five minutes, the self-doubts of that particular day. This act acknowledges them, yet doesn't allow them to interfere with the story I'm working on.

WORDPLAY #7

Here's a playful way to deal with self-doubt (confusion, fear, despair). Allow your self-doubt to speak for itself. Do it with a sense of playfulness. Write without thinking, without stopping, for five to ten minutes. I would begin this way: "I am Jean's (use your own name) self-doubt and I am persistent and powerful." Then let it tell you about itself, the areas of your life it affects, the times it makes you hesitant or fearful. Think of yourself as taking dictation. Allow your self-doubt to tell you what it wants, what it's afraid of, what it's trying to do for you, what it's protecting you from. Get to know your self-doubt; befriend it. Perhaps you and your self-doubt can find a way to coexist in a mutually beneficial way.

Begin now.

This process can be used to increase your self-knowledge in any situation where self-doubt or other kind of negative thinking is an obstacle.

WORDPLAY #8

1. Think of a favorite author, living or not, or a writer you particularly admire. Take five to ten minutes (no thinking, no stopping) to write a letter to that person; tell him or her all the things you appreciate about his or her writing. Then describe the problems you have with your writing. Ask that person for advice.

2. Take another five to ten minutes to write a reply to yourself as if it came from the writer you chose — thanking you for the compliments, and giving you constructive solutions to your writing problems.

Try this technique sometime. It may sound peculiar, but like the rest of the playful ideas in this book, it can be a powerful tool.

Chapter Fourteen

Writing Is Too Serious to Be Taken Seriously

A DIALOGUE

JEAN: You've got to be kidding. What do you mean writing is too serious to be taken seriously? Who are you, anyway?

VOICE: I am your muse; my name is Amuse. You were daydreaming, wishing for a muse to inspire you; so, here I am.

JEAN: Where did you come from?

AMUSE: From your subconscious. You wanted someone to help you keep going on this book, to help you finish it on schedule. I overheard John telling you how happily he'd worked on his book until he showed it to a friend who praised it. After she said it would be powerful, John hadn't worked on it since.

JEAN: I told him to go back to having fun with it, to forget about it having to be powerful. I reminded him of the fourth law of writing.

The fourth law of writing is:
Write for fun, for personal value.
If you don't enjoy the process, why should anyone enjoy the product?
Pleasure precedes profit.

AMUSE: So, here I am to remind you to do the same thing. You've been feeling very heavy about this *Anybody Can Write* project, very serious; and you've slowed down.

JEAN: So, tell me what you're doing here. I'm running out of time.

AMUSE: I'm the free and creative and playful part of you. I'm unconcerned about time. I usually have a mischievous appreciation of the humor of it all, and a sense of the ridiculous. Wit and Wisdom are my parents. I'm always good for a laugh, a quip, a joke. I've been criticized for being superficial, but I don't care what others think. I am self-contained, seeing both self and others with a detached and delicious humor. I have a gift for making things light and easy.

JEAN: How do you propose to make my involvement with this book light and easy?

AMUSE: My message to you is "amuse thyself" — that's what you're doing at the moment. Anything else I can do for you?

JEAN: I can't seem to seriously settle down to work today.

AMUSE: If you're determined to be serious, I can't help. What do you really want?

JEAN: I want to feel good about my writing again. I feel so shut down I can hardly breathe, but I don't know what that has to do with my book. I keep trying to stay on topic, to the point. I keep trying to honor my commitment to get this completed on time.

AMUSE: Oh dear! "On topic, to the point, commitment,

time." How grim. How limiting. How boring. You say you want to feel good. What would it take?

JEAN: I don't know. I keep going through the motions, but I'm tending to stay stuck and safe. No joy, no satisfaction, no fun. I don't like feeling so fearful and stuck.

AMUSE: Why not enjoy feeling stuck?

JEAN: How can I do that?

AMUSE: How can you not? Think about it (pardon the expression). Let's hear it for the joys of feeling stuck!

JEAN: Are you making fun of me?

AMUSE: More like making fun *for* you. I'm always on your side, but not always the side you might expect. Okay, here are your choices: (1) feeling stuck, but repressing it, (2) admitting feeling stuck, but not liking it, and (3) feeling stuck and wallowing in it, surrendering to it — even, heaven forbid, enjoying it. Your choice.

JEAN: I'll give wallowing a try. Stuck. Mired. Not breathing; no inspiration. Quiet. Safe. Stuck. Stifled; muffled; confined. No energy. No smiles. No joy. No pain. No emotions, just motions. Stuck. Truly stuck. Unmoving. Unmoved. Paralyzed. Immobile. Dead. Safe. Nothing. Stuck; stuck; stuck. Horrible word!

AMUSE: Why horrible? Stuck is a funny word.

JEAN: Funny? Nothing's fun. Nothing's funny.

AMUSE: But you just said stuck was nothing. Then you said nothing's funny. Therefore, stuck is a funny word.

JEAN: You're twisting my words.

AMUSE: One of my better skills; a harmless diversion. Twisting words and meanings and following peculiar connections. I really enjoy doing that. Now, where were we?

JEAN: I was wallowing. You weren't taking me seriously.

AMUSE: That's right. Say, why don't you write a humorous essay about writer's blocks?

JEAN: I might do it, just to see what happens.

WRITER'S BLOCKS MAKE GREAT WALLS

Here's a handy reference guide to seven of the most common writer's blocks. Very useful for identifying stuck-o walls.

Block #1 — Think Before You Write: Think about what you want to say. Think about how it better be done correctly, that it better be good and original or, at least, properly grammatical. Think about everyone who might read it — especially your mother. Get a fresh cup of coffee and think some more.

Block #2 — Do Research Instead: It's probably important that you know everything about kiwi fruit or Parisian brothels or how to stalk, kill, eviscerate, and roast a wild boar before you tackle that next chapter. Do your research in person if possible; travel is good for the writer. Don't even begin your writing until your research is complete.

Block #3 — Get Plenty of Advice: Show your first pages, or a partial draft, to your spouse or significant other, to your friends, maybe even your dentist. Ignore the fact that one definition of a camel is a horse assembled by a committee. Take all the pieces of advice you can get — even if they contradict each other. Don't trust yourself.

Block #4 — Take All Comments Personally: When your work is criticized, if they say it's not perfect, assume it's you they don't like. Pout, sulk, and complain about your unfair treatment. If you are lavishly praised, or hailed as the new Ernest Hemingway or Erma Bombeck, don't bother to rewrite or polish anything. Send it out to be published immediately and, when it's rejected, stop writing altogether.

Block #5 — Wait for Inspiration: Check your daily horoscope, and your biorhythms. If your lucky purple socks are in the wash, do the laundry instead. Organize your desk while you wait — at least you're near the typewriter; clean the keys and change the ribbon. If your muse continues to play coy, go to a movie; you may want to write a screenplay someday.

Block #6 — Procrastinate! Procrastinate!: Procrastination is a magnificent prioritizer. Just think, if you can postpone it long enough, you may not have to write it at all.

Someone else will do it or the idea will be outdated. Never write today. Tomorrow will be better.

Block #7 — Always Be Serious: Never be satisfied with less than perfection. Remember how significant what you are doing needs to be. Don't forget for one moment how much is riding on the completion of this project. If you botch it up, you could lose face, lose credibility, or lose your mind. Never quit pressuring yourself to perform. The resulting writer's cramp, or paralysis of will, usually disappears in a year or two — after the danger of success is past.

WORDPLAY #9

Have a conversation or discussion with *your* muse, or your inspiration, or inner wisdom, or writer's block. Take five to ten minutes. Write without thinking; write without stopping. Have fun.

Begin now.

Chapter Fifteen

> **Persistence and Other Useful Attitudes**

All my life I've had a love/hate affair with the word discipline; it's what I thought was necessary to be successful as a writer, or in any other worthwhile endeavor. Discipline, said the grown-ups of my world, was the main thing I needed. So I sought discipline, but never felt as if I found it — or, if I did, I couldn't keep it for long enough to make any difference.

Most of my students initially tell me that needing discipline is one of the reasons they come to a writing class. One after the other, they collectively reflect the notion that if only they were more disciplined, their success would be assured.

The truth is that disciplined people do achieve more than those who are undisciplined.

Adela Rogers St. Johns claimed that self-discipline was tremendously important in her success as a writer of bestsellers. "I stay at my typewriter through thick and thin. If I go skittering around, I'll lose the momentum of the words when they are ready to begin moving. Instead of talking or dreaming about writing, I do. When I want to tell a story, I sit down and tell it. I work very hard."

Discipline, in my experience, has a joyless quality to it. As a strong-willed person I can manage occasional periods of self-discipline. When I was completing my second book I had a lot to do in a short time. I set aside ten days; to free myself from distractions, I borrowed an empty apartment from an aunt and moved in with my computer and a sleeping bag. All I did for those ten days was walk and write and walk and write. Only one day resembled fun; to get me through the other days I made a sign to post near my computer that reminded me: *You don't have to do this forever.*

Fortunately, I ultimately discovered something better than discipline: persistence. Persistence is possible even when discipline is lacking. Although the concepts seem similar, there is a significant difference between the two. When I looked up the words in my dictionary, I was struck by the negativity of the word *discipline.* The definition of the word *persistence* just seemed more positive, more like something I really wanted.

> Discipline: 1. training to act in accordance with rules. Synonym: chastisement, castigation. See: punish, correction.
>
> Persistence: 1. to continue steadily, especially in spite of opposition. Synonym: persevering, steadfast, resolute. See: stubborn.

No wonder most of us have trouble with discipline; no wonder many of us fall short of our desires and expectations regarding issues of discipline. And who needs discipline if you are stubborn enough? Calvin Coolidge knew the value of persistence. He said:

> Press on. Nothing in the world can take the place of persistence. Talent will not; nothing is more common than unsuccessful men with talent. Genius will not; unrewarded genius is almost a proverb. Education alone will not; the world is full of educated derelicts. Persistence and determination alone are omnipotent.

Therefore, persistence is perhaps the most useful attribute you can cultivate in yourself.

The fifth law of writing is:
Write anyway.
Ignore discouraging words, internal and external.
Persistence always pays off.

Enthusiasm, passion, and Einstein's "holy curiosity" all are galvanizing, and often provide the impetus for any project, written or otherwise. Follow your passions, your enthusiasms, and your curiosity. If they sustain you throughout the writing process, you won't even need persistence. If, however, your enthusiasm dwindles, and you feel like quitting, go ahead and quit. Often I advise students: if at first you don't succeed, quit. When they argue that they can't seem to quit either, I say, "If you can't let go of the idea, can't give up the dream, or the doing, then never give up. Persist. Persevere. Keep on keeping on."

Dorothea Brande, in a self-help book first published in 1936, suggested that writers should *act as if it were impossible to fail.*

Ann Gowen Combs, a former student, used a variation of this philosophy to actualize her dream of becoming a columnist. She had been moderately successful in publishing humorous articles, mostly in the Sunday magazine sections of local newspapers. While in class, she had been writing a humorous book based on her family's experience remodeling an old house. A literary agent kept the book for a year before returning it, advising Ann that her book needed a ghost, or some sex, to be salable. Ann set the book aside to continue working on shorter pieces.

One day after class Ann told me, "What I really want is to be a columnist." She said she had already approached the two metropolitan daily newspapers in person. Since they had both published her work and knew its quality, she proposed to do a weekly column for them, similar to the humor features they had been buying from her. The editors at both papers had been cordial but firmly discouraging, saying they seldom used columns not produced by staff. Besides, so much inexpensive material was available to them through the newspaper syndicates.

Suddenly, I had a brainstorm. "Ann, are you sure you want to be a columnist?" She assured me she did. "If you really want to be a columnist," I said, "I'll tell you how to do it."

"Okay, how?" she challenged.

"It's simple. If you want to be a columnist, you do what columnists do." Ann raised one eyebrow. "Columnists write columns," I explained.

"Really?" She had a hard time keeping the sarcasm out of her voice.

I continued. "If you'll write a column every week for twenty-six weeks, I guarantee that at the end of that time you will be a columnist."

"Twenty-six weeks? Guaranteed? I'll do it," she promised.

"At the end of that time you'll have two things," I said. "First, you'll have the week in, week out *experience* of being a columnist. Second, you'll have twenty-six columns to approach a newspaper syndicate with." She looked excited by the challenge. "By the way," I added, "what newspaper do you want to write for?"

She reminded me that both newspapers had just turned her down. "Doesn't make any difference," I said. "Which paper?"

She named one; the other already had Erma Bombeck. "Okay," I said, "I'd like you to find someone, anyone, who works for that newspaper. Then, send that person a copy of your weekly column every single week, for twenty-six weeks."

She was skeptical, but willing, and she found a friend of a friend who worked for the advertising department of the newspaper. After sending him one column every week for six weeks, I suggested she call him to ask what he thought. "Well, my wife liked one of them," he reluctantly said. The second time she called him, some weeks later, he said, "I'm culling out the best to take over to the news side." The advertising and editorial departments are independent of each other, but eventually the book review editor got the buck passed to him. He finally passed along some of Ann's columns to a second editor.

My only role in this was to support her in continuing to write and send columns, and encourage her to phone each successive editor often enough that she couldn't be forgotten, but not so often that the editor would consider her a nuisance.

One morning, nineteen weeks into the campaign, she called me. "Guess what?" she asked. Although it wasn't unusual for her to call me, I was astonished when she said, "The newspaper just called. They want me to be their columnist."

"Congratulations," I said. "I knew you could do it." I had known she could do it, but I was flabbergasted because, to my knowledge, what she had accomplished had never really been done. At least not that way. I *had* been convinced that the creative principle was valid. If you want to be something, then do what that kind of person does. Act as if it were impossible to fail, keep on keeping on, and don't take no for an answer. Persistence, perseverance, stubbornness, will always win out.

One day a few months later, Ann received a letter from a New York publisher mentioning that he had seen some of her columns. "Would you, by any chance have a book?" he asked. Of course, she still had the rejected book about the home remodeling; she sent it off to him and it was eventually published *sans* ghost, *sans* sex.

"You are never given a wish," says Richard Bach in *Illusions,* "without also being given the power to make that wish come true. You may have to work for it, however." The power comes from the willingness to involve yourself persistently with whatever you wish to do or be, and to keep working toward it until it happens. *No matter what it takes.*

Part of what it takes is commitment — to yourself, to the dream of writing, or of being a columnist, novelist, poet, or whatever; and commitment to an idea, to giving that idea life on paper. Commitment is a measurable thing. It is not what you said you were going to do, or what you planned to do, or what you would like to happen. Commitment is what you actually *did.* Results determine commitment, not the other way around. Look at what you are doing, what you are actually accomplishing, to discover what you're committed to.

Chapter Sixteen

The Trial-and-Error-and-Error-and-Error Method

Whether you decide to write for your own satisfaction, for self-discovery, as an escape, as an outlet for your own creativity, or for publication, the learning process is seldom as straightforward as most of us have been led to believe. Among my more persistent notions about writing is that it should become easier the longer I keep at it. The truth is that some things have become easier to accomplish; however, my standards and goals have escalated also, so there's always a sense of stretching or even impossibility.

I often used to feel that I wasted a lot of writing time with things that didn't work out. I'd begin a story, lose interest, try it again later — maybe from a different point of view. Sometimes I'd even rewrite it several times, but still not be satisfied enough to submit it for publication. I kept hoping I could streamline my process, waste less time, and raise my batting average of pieces submitted and sold. In my fantasy I would sit down to write and the right words would pour out the end of my pen, all ready to polish into a final manuscript. No false starts. No abortive ideas. No endless rewriting. But my reality didn't measure up to my fantasy.

I'd been taught to plan my writing carefully, to do an outline and stick to that outline. Bor-ing! Instead, I would wander off in strange directions chasing a renegade idea — sometimes never returning to my original design. Occasionally, derailed in exploring other possibilities, I ended up with a successful piece with little resemblance to what I'd planned to do. Years later, I realized that those unplanned pieces, *because* they were unplanned, allowed me to access the creativity that usually eluded me when I tried too hard to control the process.

Nevertheless, I felt guilty about deviating from the plan, until I heard of something called the "correction model." First, you do it; then, you correct it. All my life I'd used that approach to learning, but thought I was wrong. I wasn't wrong; a person learns by doing, by experiencing, then fixing it if necessary, but always learning *something* in the process. The trial-and-error-and-error-and-error process for writing works just fine. Nothing is wasted either, since something is learned from each try, each error.

The sixth law of writing is:
Write a lot. Use everything.
Learning comes from your own struggles with
words on paper.

I discovered an important fact about what shows up in print. Most books, stories, and articles in print represent maybe ten percent of the words the writer produced on the subject. The writing, rewriting, and editing process removes a large percentage of the original output if you count from where the project started as an idea on the back of an envelope down to the final draft. And every single word, including the ones edited out, are useful.

Consider the iceberg below. The part that shows above the waterline only hints at the massive and stabilizing underwater foundation. Published stories, articles, and books are similar. The material (sometimes as much as ninety percent) that ends up lost, or edited out, somehow validates the part

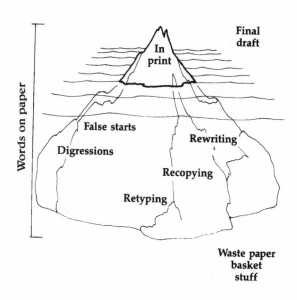

that shows up in print. Although it may not be visible, the knowledgeable eye can tell the difference between an ice floe and an iceberg. Similarly, the discriminating editor or reader can tell the difference between a piece of writing that was just dashed off and one that has evolved, having been stabilized and supported by all the words thrown away.

Although I used to feel discouraged about discarded words and phrases and sentences and paragraphs and pages, I gradually learned to appreciate the usefulness of this natural selection process. In talking to other writers, including successful authors who have been publishing for years, I learned that there is a wide variety in the ratio of words written to words published. Some writers do a lot of sorting, the trial-and-error stuff, in their heads; some who claim to do only one or two drafts will admit that their process has not always been so efficient. Most writers' apprenticeships resulted in a great quantity of unpublished words, and many writers have simply forgotten how it was when they first began writing.

The write-without-thinking system I advocate does tend to produce more digressions, more unused (or unusable) words and pages than other, more disciplined approaches. Nevertheless, unless you already have a system for writing that satisfies you, the trial-and-error method will definitely work. Your output will increase, as will your pleasure in the doing, thereby increasing the possibilities of ultimate success. This route to success in writing may appear to be a longer, less-traveled path, but the destination is often the same.

Your investment of time and energy in this sort of creative exploration is risky. You take the chance that the result will be merely a learning experience, which some people regard as failure. Risking failure is a difficult undertaking since most of us fear failure; most of all, we fear being seen as a failure. Failure, however, is an event — not a person. I can fail to bring my story to a satisfying conclusion, and I can fail to get it published, but neither of those things makes me a failure. If I'm determined to learn from my experiences with writing, from my trials and errors, then nothing is a failure — all is learning.

Interestingly enough, my failures — those efforts that did not result in satisfaction — were usually much more powerful learning experiences than those that did succeed. For example, when I first began taking writing classes I thought I *should* write children's stories. After all, I did have four children, and I was depriving them of my caretaking two nights a week to attend class. Therefore, if I wrote a story for each one of them, I could justify spending time and energy writing. Although today's consciousness about parenthood seems more enlightened, I still encounter students, both men and women, who feel they must justify their involvement with writing for similar reasons and in similar ways.

During my first quarter in writing class I dutifully created four stories, one for each of my children. Despite the fact that my children enjoyed the stories, the pieces failed in class and failed to get published. I wrote half a dozen more of them before I realized that I didn't know enough about being a child, about the playfulness of childhood. In my own growing-up years, I had been rewarded for being serious, and became a pseudo-adult at an early age. Reviewing my so-called children's stories now, I see why they didn't work. They were heavy on moralizing with a parental agenda rather than a more appropriate, childlike viewpoint. And, suitably enough, I hadn't enjoyed the writing of them; for me they had been only a duty.

Although I failed in my goal of writing children's stories, the time was not wasted; I gained self-knowledge and learned what I didn't need to write any more. In addition, I pleased my children. Since that was my true intention anyway, it might have been more useful to question my ambition to publish the stories. I also learned that I always need to work on ideas that are important to me; I learned not to get sidetracked by my *should write* projects; I learned I needed to please myself with my writing, not other people.

Somerset Maugham reflected his self-knowledge when he wrote:

> I discovered my limitations, and it seemed to me that the only sensible thing to do was to aim at what excellence I could within them. I knew I had no lyrical quality. I had a small vocabulary and no efforts that I could make to enlarge it much availed me. I

had little gift of metaphor. The original and striking simile seldom occurred to me. Poetic flights and the great imaginative sweep were beyond my powers. I was tired of doing what did not come easily to me. On the other hand, I had an acute power of observation, and it seemed to me that I could see a great many things that other people missed. I could put down in clear terms what I saw. I had a logical sense, and if no great feeling for the richness or strangeness of words, at all events I knew that I could never write as well as I could wish, but I thought with pains I could arrive at writing as well as my natural defects allowed.

Isn't honesty appealing?

WRITING EXERCISE #3
SELF-KNOWLEDGE INTERVIEW

Here are some questions you might ask yourself when uncertainty about a writing project stalls your forward progress.

1. Who am I writing this for?
2. Am I excited about working on it?
3. Am I doing it primarily for myself?
4. How important is it for me to explore this on paper?

5. Is this the right time to write this story?
6. Do I passionately believe in what I'm writing?
7. Am I willing to explore this idea in writing to the best of my ability?
8. Will I invest enough time on a regular basis to explore this until I complete a first rough draft?
9. Can I let go of all expectations or demands for perfection from myself?
10. Am I willing to risk writing this no matter what happens?
11. Am I determined to enjoy the success of my creative exploration, or the opportunity for self-knowledge?

If you answered yes to most of these questions, there's no way you can fail, no way you cannot find value in the trial-and-error-and-error-and-error method of writing.

These questions are not meant to discourage experimentation. Your apprenticeship years are when you can try out different kinds of writing, both fiction and nonfiction. The only way you can find out what sort of writing you might be best at is to try many different forms of writing that interest you. If you enjoy attending plays or movies, try writing a stage play or a screenplay. Write both nonfiction articles and invented stories to see which might be easiest, which might bring the most satisfaction.

Chapter Seventeen

Accessing Both Past and Future

Although writing is very much a here and now action, knowing how to gain access to the past and use it appropriately can enrich your stories; knowing how to capitalize on daydreaming and fantasies of the future can facilitate your writing efforts as well.

This essay, written in 1823 by Ludwig Borne, still speaks eloquently to today's would-be writer:

There are men and books that teach Latin, Greek, or French in three days, and bookkeeping in only three hours. So far however, no one has offered a course on How to Become a Good Original Writer in Three Days. And yet, it's so easy! There is nothing to learn, but plenty to unlearn; nothing to acquire, but much to forget. Every human mind is born with beautiful ideas — new ideas, too, since in every human being the world is created anew. But life and education write their useless stuff over them and cover them up.

To see things as they really are, consider this: We know an animal, a fruit, a flower in their true shape; they appear to us the way they are. But would anyone understand the true nature of a chicken, an apple tree, or a rose if he knew only chicken pie, apple sauce, or rose perfume? And yet, that's all we ever get in the sciences, and in anything that we take in through our minds rather than our senses. It comes to us changed and made up; we need to know it in its raw, naked form. Thinking is the kitchen where all truths are killed, plucked, cut up, fried, and pickled. What we need most today are unthinking books — books with things in them rather than thoughts.

There are only very few original writers. Our best writers differ from the poorer ones far less than you might think. One writer creeps to his goal, another runs, a third hobbles, a fourth dances, a fifth drives, a sixth rides on horseback: but the goal and the road are common to all. Great new ideas are found only in solitude: but where is solitude to be found? You can get away from people — and at once you are in the noisy marketplace of books; you can throw away all the books, too; but how do you clear the mind of all the conventional ideas that education has poured into it? The true art of self-training is the art of making yourself ignorant: the finest and most useful of the arts and one that is rarely and poorly practiced.

The true search for knowledge is not like the voyage of Columbus but like that of Ulysses. Man is born abroad, living means seeking your home, and thinking means living. But the home of ideas is the heart; if you want fresh water, you must draw from the source; the mind is but a river, on whose banks live thousands who muddy its waters by washing, bathing, flax steeping, and other dirty business. The mind is the arm, the heart is the will. Strength can be acquired, increased, and trained, but what good is strength without the courage to use it? A cowardly fear of thinking curbs us all; the censorship of public opinion is more oppressive than that of governments. Most writers are no better than they are because they have ideas, but no character. Their weakness comes from vanity. They want to surpass their fellow writers, but to surpass someone you must meet him on his own ground, to overtake someone you must travel the same road. That's why the good writers have so much in common with the bad ones: the good one is like the bad one, but a little bit bigger; he goes in the same direction, but a little farther.

To be original, you must listen to the voice of your heart rather than the clamor of the world — and have the courage to teach publicly what you have learned. The source of all genius is sincerity;

men would be wiser if they were more moral.

And now comes the application that I promised: Take several sheets of paper and for three days in succession, without any pretense or hypocrisy, write down everything that comes to your mind. Write what you think about yourself, about women, about the Turkish War, the Fonk Trial, about the Last Judgment, about your boss — and after three days you will be beside yourself with surprise at all the new unheard-of ideas you had. That's the art of becoming an original writer in three days!

Although some of the historical references are outdated, you can easily substitute today's headlines to bring them up to date. Borne's method, which Freud claims was the basis for psychoanalysis, is a simple and wise process for letting go of outmoded thoughts and stale habits. Borne's method can also generate some ideas worth playing with — ideas that reside in your storehouse of experience.

"The true art of self-training," Borne calls it. That's what writing really is; self-training is certainly what this book and my workshops are all about. I fervently hope you will take the time to follow his simple suggestions for "making yourself ignorant."

Now, let's move from 1823 to the future. The following process is versatile; it can be used both to contemplate your future and to gain access to your past.

WORDPLAY #10

Let's begin with a future fantasy. Mentally move yourself ahead two years (or five, or ten). What is the year, month, day? How old will you be then? As you project yourself ahead two years in time, explore on paper your fantasy of how you would like your life to be. Where would you like to be living? With whom? What changes have occurred for you in the past two years? How do you feel about those changes in your life? What are you doing that you've always dreamed of doing? What is your involvement with writing? This is a chance to try on any of your dreams for size. Write anything you like, as long as you write as if it were happening today. Reminder: all Wordplay exercises work best if you approach them as just-for-fun, playful word games — games where you get points for words on paper.

Once again: *Write without thinking; write without stopping.* Write for ten to fifteen minutes; set a timer if you need to. *Write in the present tense.* Write as if it were that future date today and those things were happening now. Begin your writing by stating the date and how old you are in this future time: "It is . . . and I am. . . ."

Enjoy. Begin now.

This exercise is simply a projection into the future. If you can visualize or imagine an event happening on paper, it's more likely to come to pass. This technique can enable you to tap into your subconscious and bring more into your conscious awareness. Projection into the future can also be used to explore options. When confronted with a choice you're unsure about, you can project ahead a few months or a few years into the future for each option. Try out your decisions on paper instead of thinking about them. Write until something surprises you.

This approach can also be used to sort out ideas to write about, especially book ideas. Pretend that your book is finished; fantasize what is happening as a result of its completion. How do your friends and family feel about your achievement? Again, write until something surprises you.

WORDPLAY #11

Time projection can enable you to visit or re-experience the past, any time in your past. You can use incidents or emotions from the past to provide *truth* for your articles or stories.

Choose a specific date or season of the year (the day I began seventh grade, my tenth birthday, or the summer I fell in love for the first time). Be as specific as possible. Put down as many details about your surroundings as you can — your family, your friends and other people, pets, the circumstances of your life. Write for ten to fifteen minutes.

Begin now. Write in the present tense, as if things were happening minute by minute as you write. Stay in the present tense.

There's a profound difference in both the quality and quantity of output between that which is recollected ("I remember when . . .") and that which is re-experienced ("It's my tenth birthday today and I hope I'm going to get a party"). Because memory is filtered through the critic, what Freud called "the censor of the mind," our recollections are often distorted. Try to gain access to the past both ways, first through remembering, and then by re-experiencing it, just to prove the difference to yourself. Play around with this idea. When you imagine that something from the past is happening now, in the present, your words flow from the creative and childlike part of you, the part that knows how to pretend.

What happens on paper as a result of this method will probably be neither totally accurate nor profound — but somewhere in the words and pages produced will be something you didn't know before, something useful, or something surprising. You may only discover this later, when you read over what you wrote, rather than during the time you're actually writing. Perhaps you'll be surprised by an insight, or a feeling, or just something amusing. You'll never know until you try.

Chapter Eighteen

Finding Time to Write

"Where do you find the time to write?" students often ask. They protest that their jobs, or school, or family obligations leave little time to write on a regular basis. They say they will write more when they graduate, or when their children start school, or leave for college, or when they retire.

First I tell them: *"People make room in their lives for what is important to them."* I've learned that when I have something I passionately want to say, I get it done no matter how busy I think I am. Besides, if you're not actualizing your dream of writing *now,* in some small way, it may never happen. If what you want to write is important enough, you'll be able to find the time. And if you don't find the time, consider looking for a more important story to write.

The seventh law of writing is:
Write out of commitment to your ideas,
commitment to yourself as a writer.
Trust yourself.

Set aside a regular time for your writing, not necessarily on a daily basis, but certainly on a consistent basis. Even in my busiest weeks, my aim is to take action, to move forward, on my current writing project; during any given week, I want to accumulate manuscript pages, to write something — even if it's wrong. So, I schedule my time to write. As little as one-and-a-half hours a week will keep some momentum going on my project. And I make sure that time is spent *writing* — sprawling words onto paper. Writing is a measurable endeavor, measurable in terms of pages or, better yet, word count.

Remember that three-part writing exercise at the end of Chapter Eleven? I hope you took the time to do it. If not, go back and do it now, or skip ahead to do the three-part exercise at the end of this chapter, or set your timer for exactly fifteen minutes and write steadily about anything at all until the timer goes off. The next idea will be much more useful for you if you work from a personal point of reference. Whichever fifteen-minute writing sample you use, go back and count the number of words from beginning to end. Then, double that total. The final bit of math is to multiply that doubled total by 260.

What you will end up with as a result of your calculations is the number of words you would accumulate on paper if you wrote for half an hour a day, five days a week, for a year. Usually, the sum is well over 100,000 words. Only 500 words a day, for instance, when multiplied by 260 equals 130,000 words. Most books published today contain between 60,000 and 100,000 words — typical for novels. Nonfiction and children's books sometimes contain less than 25,000 words. Even after considering the iceberg model, where a large percentage gets thrown out or edited away, half an hour a day, five days a week, could produce a significant number of final draft words in a year.

I admit that this kind of writing often produces a very raggedy first draft — zero-draft stuff. However, half an hour a day, five days a week, even in the busiest life, *is* achievable. If you are, indeed, putting words on paper that entire half-hour, you can think about your story later when you're doing the dishes, or driving to work, or out for a walk, and you'll end up with pages you wouldn't otherwise have accomplished.

During that half-hour, it really doesn't matter what you write as long as it's even vaguely related to the subject or story or idea you've chosen. All of the work will be useful in the sense that it will feed the dream of writing, and it will feed the writing that follows. Your daily writing period will create the continuity and involvement that you want and need. Anthony Trollope said, "A small daily task, if it be really daily, will beat the labors of a spasmodic Hercules." Trollope also said, "Three to four hours a day is as much as any writer needs to do if he is indeed writing during that time."

The daily output from this writing time will be different for each individual, as will the time it will take to complete a first or final draft. To think only in terms of word or page count, however, may lead to feeling overwhelmed by the numbers. You may lose the sense of fun, the excitement and creativity. I used to feel I could never write a book, until I learned that a book was written just like anything else, one page at a time, and all I really had to concern myself with was today's page or pages. That everyday quota, however, was vital to the fulfillment of my dream.

Although a lot of time is not required at first, a regular involvement with your writing on a week to week basis is beneficial. As little as two to three hours *weekly* will advance your dream of writing; but you must protect that time from intrusions and distractions. For years I wrote at home with four children underfoot and a husband who never hesitated to interrupt my work. I longed for a room of my own — a room to write in. Then we moved and I finally had a separate room for my desk and electric typewriter; husband and kids still traipsed in and out. I often complained that my family didn't take my writing seriously. Years later, I realized that it had been me that hadn't taken my writing seriously enough to protect it properly. I seldom closed my office door, and never asked them to respect my writing time. Today, I'd post a sign on my closed office door announcing: *Writer at Work. Interrupt only for breathing or bleeding emergencies.*

Annie Dillard was asked about her Pulitzer Prize–winning book, *Pilgrim at Tinker Creek.* Where did she find the time to write? After all, wasn't she a housewife? Her answer:

I don't do housework. Life is too short, and I'm too much of a Puritan. If you want to take a year to write a book, you have to take that year, or the year will take you by the hair and pull you toward the grave. Let the grass die. I let almost all of my indoor plants die from neglect while I was writing the book. There are all kinds of ways to live. You can take your choice. You can keep a tidy house, and when St. Peter asks you what you did with your life, you can say, I kept a tidy house, I made my own cheese balls.

Time to write, therefore, is always a matter of priority. I eventually learned that the question of time also includes the energy factor. Different tasks in writing need different kinds of time and energy. Journal writing, for example, can be done on demand, unless I'm processing intense emotions, in which case I need not only protected time, but also privacy. First-draft creative work needs prime time, the maximum energy time of my day, the time I feel the freshest. I used to be a night owl, and wrote best late at night after the house was quiet. Later, I wrote when the children were napping or at school. Eventually, I found I needed to schedule my creative-stage writing in the morning, before anything else claimed my attention.

Medium-energy tasks, like rewriting, could be scheduled for afternoons or evenings. Some days, I discovered, were low-energy days from the outset; those were the times I did filing and sorting, but very little else. Learn to assess your energy level when scheduling writing time, lest you set yourself up for disappointment. Dr. Hans Selye said:

> Every person has his own natural stress level at which his mind and body function most efficiently. Any forced deviation from this natural baseline may have ill effects. In other words, it is just as bad to restrain a naturally active energetic person from going at his own intense pace as it is to drive a passive, bucolic individual to attempt peak accomplishment.

Another kind of self-knowledge will also help you devise a realistic schedule. How do you get tasks done? Are you a daily routine person, or a deadline worker? Deadline workers are often very efficient in their own manic way, but suffer from guilt or accusations of procrastinating. Procrastination has a bad reputation in the traditional world, where tasks are evaluated, but if you dependably get important tasks done, you are well advised to drop the guilt and use your self-knowledge to your advantage. If you are genuinely a binge artist, a wait-until-the-last-minute-then-bang-it-out kind of person, plan a weekly writing binge or two, rather than try for a more regular — and personally incompatible — schedule. What the world calls procrastination can be a useful prioritizer. Don't try to change your style. Remember: *If it works, don't fix it.*

Also, if a writing schedule is a new habit for you and you forget and miss a day or two, don't think you'll then have to do several days' writing all at once. If, for whatever reason, you miss a day, just skip it. You do not have to make it up, and feeling guilty will only interfere with fun — which is the primary purpose of early writing, first-stage writing, creative writing. Never lose sight of the pleasure you can derive from spending time writing a story that has personal value for you.

WRITING EXERCISE #4
TIME AND MONEY

Set aside fifteen to twenty minutes for this three-part exercise using the projection technique. Once again, don't forget to write without thinking, without stopping. Have fun.

1. Write from the point of view of your wristwatch, or the clock you're using to time this exercise. Or choose a favorite clock. Allow the timepiece to describe itself and how it influences your life; let it refer to you by your first name. Let the timepiece comment about how you respond to deadlines, or handle time in general. Begin now.

2. Now, write from the viewpoint of your checkbook, wallet, or credit card. Allow the object you've chosen to tell you about itself, to say what it is most afraid of, and to comment about your relationship with money, success, or ambition.

3. Next, record a discussion between the watch or clock and the object that symbolizes money. The subject for discussion is the following fantasy: You have just won a writers' lottery. Your prize is more time or more money. Your challenge is to decide which you prefer. Allow the timepiece and the wallet to speculate about the meaning of this writers' lottery; ask them to advise you which prize they think you should choose, and why.

THE SEVEN LAWS OF WRITING

1. To write is an active verb. Thinking is not writing.
Writing is putting words
on paper.
2. Write passionately. Everybody has loves
and hates; even quiet people lead passionate lives.
Creativity follows passion.
3. Write honestly. Risk nakedness. Originality equals
vulnerability.
4. Write for fun, for personal value.
If you don't enjoy the process,
why should anyone enjoy the product?
Pleasure precedes profit.
5. Write anyway. Ignore discouraging words, internal
and external.
Persistence always pays off.
6. Write a lot. Use everything.
Learning comes from your own struggles
with words on paper.
7. Write out of commitment to your ideas,
commitment to yourself as a writer.
Trust yourself.

Part Four

Anybody Can Keep Writing

"To be any good as a writer you have to write
at least a thousand words a day every day.
That's just to keep the junk out of your system.
We all carry around too much junk —
we're all walking wounded — and you have to
get rid of it to find the good stuff.
Writing is just like athletics.
You have to keep in shape. I think
those thousand words do that."

— Ray Bradbury
Interview in *Writer's Digest*

Chapter Nineteen

The Write-Brain Experience

Understanding how your brain works when faced with the challenge of telling a story can help you keep on writing. The two-stage writing process roughly compares to right-brain/left-brain research. First-stage writing reflects the experiential characteristics of the emotional right brain: fun, sensation, intuition, imagination, spontaneity, and primitive expression. Second-stage writing takes advantage of the documented strengths of the intellectual left brain: discipline, focus, logic, judgment, wit, and precision of language. The right brain sees things happening, perceiving the large picture with no sense of the passage of time; the left brain thinks things through, providing specific details while setting and keeping schedules.

Writing students seem to fall into two corresponding categories: (1) Those whose production of pages is small and labored — "tight and constipated," one man complained. Their writing is logical in concept, mechanically correct, but often sterile in feeling. These left-brain students are well organized, skill oriented, and excel in presenting facts, but

143

often have difficulty writing fiction. (2) The others, usually a smaller group, tend to produce an abundance of messy pages. These right-brain individuals love the process, the act of writing, but have problems figuring out how to organize their pages into a satisfying and coherent whole; they play fast and loose with facts, and avoid outlining.

Writing classes and workshops not only give each group exposure to the strengths of the other group, but also offer the opportunity to practice the skills each lacks. Left-brain writers need to loosen up, to put their critical judgmental selves aside while they write and write and write. Right-brain writers need to break down the job of organization by focusing on small tasks that allow them to discriminate between what serves their story and what needs to be left out.

Good writers, successful writers, have both right- and left-brain abilities. Many highly successful writers enjoy an unconscious cooperation between the two sides of their brains; others develop the ability to allow a back and forth, free flow of energy as they switch from right-brain duties to left-brain ones and back again in writing and editing their stories and books.

Although the right brain is rumored to be nonverbal and therefore not an appropriate place from which to write seriously, the right brain does generate language; the right brain whispers and moans and screams the excitable language of emotion, where the words are primitive and the vocabulary unsophisticated. This fact tells us why most of us are unhappy with our first drafts.

The necessity for emotional integrity, however, validates the crude verbal expression of first-stage, right-brain writing. Knowing we can rely on the left brain to add precision of language and clarity of thought during the rewriting stage can help us withhold judgment throughout the all-important first draft.

If you are right-brain dominant, your writing enjoys an image-rich fluidity; you have a sense of flow, of oneness with the material. If you are left-brain dominant, you have a passion for precision that can only be satisfied during the rewriting process. Practice is required to encourage the Ping-Pong game the two sides of your brain play, to enable your writing to benefit from both fluidity and precision; it is a gradual learning experience.

I used to feel frustrated because I could recite the principles of good writing yet couldn't produce pages that reflected that knowledge. I thought there was something wrong with me until I realized that there is always a time gap between my intellectual perception of a technique and my ability to execute it. The fine tuning of an idea is a process of integration during which the right and left brains work in harmony with each other.

The following scenario illustrates the write-brain experience, where the right and left sides of the brain share writing tasks:

Right brain says: "Wow! What a great idea." Idea spark plus intuitive connection equals excitement.

Left brain agrees: "Sounds like a possible book." It

begins making notes on the back of an envelope.

Right brain begins fingerpainting with words, having fun playing around with the bits and pieces, feeding energy into nonlinear doodling and fuzzy language.

Left brain decides to play along for a while; it organizes ideas and notes, makes a list of tasks, and sets up a schedule. Linear development proceeds.

Right brain sees things happening, and explores the sensory, emotional, and imaginative possibilities in a flurry of high excitement and creativity.

Left brain reads over pages and notes, and commits to the completion of a first draft.

Right brain sprawls a zero-draft mass of words onto paper, making connections and generating surprises with raw material. Eventually it runs out of energy, and calls the left brain in for a consultation.

Left brain evaluates the sprawling first draft, decides it's worth the long-term investment of time to rewrite, makes suggestions for structural changes, gives directions for rewrite, and rearranges the material in a logical form using cut-and-paste techniques.

Right brain and left brain collaborate in an ongoing orgy of rewriting, rewriting, and more rewriting.

Left brain decides when it's time to edit and ruthlessly cuts away digressions and repetitive or dead words while upgrading the language for precision and clarity; it also kills your *darlings* — those self-indulgent phrases you love that don't serve the story.

Right brain looks at the book as a whole and asks, "How does it feel? Is it satisfying? Are the elements and parts in balance?" If not, it brainstorms about how to fix things.

Left brain organizes a final draft manuscript, polishes and fine tunes the language, uses a dictionary to check spellings and definitions. And, if the book is to be marketed, the left brain researches publishers and devises strategies for publication. The right brain aids in creative marketing.

Chapter Twenty

Lights, Camera, Action

F ocus on the writer (close-up shot). Writer paces the floor looking preoccupied. Smiles to self from time to time; chuckles aloud, rummages around for a pen, and grabs a spiral notebook. Sits down to write. Scribbles a few sentences, stares into space, frowns, leaps to feet, and resumes pacing. Jots ideas down in notebook midstride. Sits at desk and begins to write in earnest. An hour and a half later the writer looks up and can't believe how much time has disappeared.

A lot of things happen simultaneously when we approach the desk to write. The left-brain part of us that has scheduled this writing time says, "Sit down. Sit still. Get to work. You've got a thousand words to write today. Hurry up. Settle down. Stop dawdling." This is the nagging voice of the taskmaster.

The part of us that needs and wants to play with the idea — to produce an experimental zero draft — resists sitting still, detests being ordered around, avoids anything that sounds like work. This right brain, the creative part of us, is usually excited, intensely curious, and fascinated by just about everything. Although it wants to express its excitement in words on paper, it's often impatient with the time it takes. This creative child, mentally and physically restless, wriggles and fidgets and paces.

Nevertheless, once it gets started, the creative child becomes so absorbed in the activity — romping on the paper playground with ideas and words — that time disappears. The here-and-now writing experience is everything; nothing else exists. Eating and sleeping and the demands of so-called normal life represent intrusions into creative space.

Original writing, the first draft of anything, is a collaboration between the taskmaster and the creator. The taskmaster handles logistics: first it organizes the schedule, then it disciplines its need to control — and bows out temporarily for the sake of the end product. The taskmaster must voluntarily surrender to the chaos of the fun-loving creator, who refuses to perform in a linear, logical way. The creator prefers to scatter words around with a crude vitality. The intelligent taskmaster, however, knows that crude vitality is the magic ingredient, and knows that thinking cannot produce crude vitality and emotional integrity. Therefore, the taskmaster lets go, knowing that later it will have the opportunity to run quality control on the job as a whole.

People who claim they can only write when they are inspired are those who wait for the child to get excited in the presence of paper and pencil. The taskmaster has learned that the child will write at prearranged times if it's allowed to do its fretting and wriggling on paper without supervision. The taskmaster stands guard over the time, whether fifteen minutes or three hours; it sets up a realistic schedule, then lets the child roam free, saying: "Here are your toys — your paper and pencil. Do whatever you want. I'll let you know when you can go outside to play."

The child may squirm and fret, but eventually will settle down to have fun with whatever is available. As it begins to play with the words, stuff sprawls onto paper in a nonlinear brainstorm. Maybe one-tenth will be usable, but it's a vital tenth, and the proportion of good stuff to digressive output is normal and natural. Mark Harris, short-story writer and writing teacher, articulates this creative process:

> Writing comes very hard for me. I do not understand why people think writing is easy. I am at a loss to know how to arrive at Word One, much less the whole piece. Seeking a first line, I pound the typewriter very fast to start with, not for speed but for structure and discovery. I cut in on my facts at any point, haphazard, confident that something will lead to something and eventually to a beginning, by which time the work I've done up ahead will inform the work behind. Begin anywhere. Most beginning writers cannot go forward because they insist on making every sentence clean before going on to the

next. Somehow, I learned to live with the chaos of a first draft.

D. T. Suzuki, the Zen master, stated it even more succinctly. "Cultivate in yourself a good similarity to the chaos of the universe surrounding you." Chaos is one thing, boredom another. Many writers report stages of feeling so bored with the process that they end up postponing, prolonging, or abandoning their projects. Forward movement ceases.

I recently encountered a definition of boredom that resonated in me: *Boredom is rage spread thin.* I feel enraged when the initial excitement dwindles away and disappears; I feel as if I've just awakened from a dream, wondering, "Where am I?" I look at what my creative frenzy has produced. I think, "What is this junk that I've been wasting my time on?" I feel angry, duped, discouraged; I want to tear up all the pages I've done and throw them away. American novelist F. Scott Fitzgerald said, "Boredom is not an end product — it is, comparatively, rather an early stage in life and in art. You've got to go by, or past, or through boredom, as through a filter, before the clear product emerges." And novelist Irving Wallace admitted, "Starting to write a new book — especially the first few pages, before I get to know the characters, bores me. After fifty pages, the tedium wears off."

So the antidote to boredom, like many of the difficulties associated with writing, is to acknowledge it, and then keep writing until you break through to another level of excitement, creativity, or surprise. Surprises arise when your writing expresses emotional authenticity. To achieve this authenticity, it is important to distinguish between intellectual *concept* and *experience* rooted in feelings.

Read through the following zero drafts of the same incident.

First Version: Two months ago, a friend of mine committed suicide. I found myself at first feeling responsible for what happened to him. Wondering what I could have done differently. Finally realizing that I could only be responsible for myself. That it was an illusion that I really could have done anything to keep him from doing what he did. I had to free myself of the expectations that I could have saved him, or could play rescuer to save his widow from her pain. But all I could do was to deal with my own feelings of loss, go through my own grieving process.

Second Version: A friend of mine killed himself two months ago. He parked by the side of the road near his house and put a bullet through his head. A phone call woke me in the middle of the night — a mutual friend who knew I cared. I wanted to rush right over. To do something. To comfort the friend who had called. But I just hung up the phone and crawled back into my sleeping bag feeling sick and lonely. I curled up into a ball and rocked myself back and forth. Kept thinking there was something I could have or should have done so he wouldn't have needed to do that. Somehow, I'd let him down. And I was angry at him for going away, for doing that to me. I rocked myself a long, long time. I tried to comfort myself. I wondered what I could possibly say to comfort his wife, and the boys. I felt very lost and very alone. And I wanted not to feel so alone.

Notice the difference between left-brain *concept* in the first version, and right-brain *feeling* in the second one. The latter is closer to the direct experience and it avoids conceptual words like suicide, responsibility, illusion, expectation, loss, and grieving process. Analytical words such as those, words that *explain* feelings rather than *show* experiences, distance the reader. This is why writers are often advised to *show, don't tell.*

Chapter Twenty-One

Collaborating with the Subconscious

Experiencing, feeling, and seeing reflect the influence of the right brain. The essence of the creative mode is *allowing*. Not pushing, shoving, striving, or making things happen, but allowing ideas to ebb and flow and sprawl into being on the page. Many authors try to explain the source of their inspiration; one claims to see things happening, another reports that stories run like movies in her head. According to American writer Annie Dillard:

> There is another kind of seeing that involves a kind of letting go. When I see this way I sway transfixed and emptied. The difference between the two ways of seeing is the difference between walking with and without a camera. When I walk with a camera I walk from shot to shot, reading the light on a calibrated meter. When I walk without a camera, my own shutter opens, and the moment's light prints on my own silver gut. When I see this second way I am above all, an unscrupulous observer.

Most attempts to explain what goes on with the right brain fall short because it is always a personal, emotional happening. Words inadequately explain right-brain functioning, since *your* experience of the creative mode may feel different from that of anyone else. For most novelists, it's familiar territory. For others, it's a foreign country.

My first encounter — as an adult and a writer — with that rich visual realm inside my own head was deliberately planned. One spring, I'd been playing in fits and starts with an idea for a book based on my adventures as a divorcée. I began several first chapters and developed fictional characters for a somewhat autobiographical novel. Then, I outlined a nonfiction approach and tried it as an advice book, to share what I'd learned along the way. Returning to the novel form, I tried using first person, then third person; the work did not progress either way. My self-imposed, zero-draft schedule wasn't working either.

At that time I lived a complex and intense life full of verbal interaction and much involvement with the written word: leading writing workshops, evaluating student manuscripts, and preparing handouts for classes. I lectured and advised; I wrote in my personal journal, making lists and notes for stories I had neither the time nor energy to develop. For relaxation I read avidly and talked a lot with friends and students.

My friend, Janet, suggested that maybe I needed a vacation from words. Perhaps the only way I could achieve clarity, could discover the right approach for my novel to be, was to unhook from words, to wangle a temporary divorce of sorts. The idea appealed to my sense of adventure. I planned a six-day solo camping trip; I would take no written material. No books, magazines, newspapers, or manuscripts. No pens or pencils or paper to write on, not even my journal. The decision to leave my journal behind pained me; it had been my solace and daily companion for years.

Further, I would avoid talking to anyone during those six days. I would risk being alone with myself and my very busy multitrack head. I did not know for sure what would happen to this compulsive reader-writer-talker without any of the usual outlets for that energy. I borrowed a camper van, packed a minimum of food and supplies, and drove off to a state park on an island not too far away, a place both reasonably safe and remote. I expected to endure a crazed withdrawal from the world of words; I would allow myself to see what emerged, hoping to make myself new, in a sense. I was courting a new strategy for my novel — in search of a direct route to my subconscious.

After a two-hour drive from my house, I parked near a grove of fir trees on the edge of an old apple orchard, a causeway my only link with the mainland. It was mid-May and unusually decent weather for the Pacific Northwest. The snow-capped Olympic Mountains jutted skyward to the west, and the rocky beach of Jarrel's Cove was a two-minute walk from my campsite. The afternoon, sunny but not too warm, stretched interminably before me. I looked around the deserted campground. Nothing to do. Nothing to read. No paper. No pencil. Nothing to do but walk; so that's what I did.

I walked several miles along the beach, down to the point and back. Explored nearby roads, then returned to camp, built a fire, and cooked a simple dinner the hard way; it took longer that way and I had plenty of time. No evening newspaper, no television, no manuscripts to critique. I walked the beach again, more slowly this time. I returned near dusk, my jacket pockets heavy with pretty-colored rocks, sand dollars, and bits of driftwood. I arranged them in a pleasing pattern on a slab of wood and crawled into my sleeping bag exhausted.

Crows in raucous chorus awakened me at daylight. I couldn't sleep anyway — my overactive head had already kicked into gear. I got up, dressed, and ate breakfast all by 6:30, definitely not the norm for me. What to do? No things-to-do-today list. No journal to confide in. No letters to answer. It was impossible to sit still without paper of some sort in my hands. The extent of my addiction became clearer; I craved a book, a manuscript, my spiral notebook, scratch paper — anything.

I explored the island and encountered a deer; two king-fishers dipped and screeched, circling overhead. I found a wooded piece of property with a weathered For Sale sign — a perfect place for a writers' colony. I sat and daydreamed awhile. Then, restless, I walked and walked and walked; I must have walked six to eight hours that day. Finally, I took off my watch and put it in the glove compartment of the van. Over the next few days, I still felt an ache for my notebook, something to write on, something to read, someone to talk with. It diminished, over time, but never disappeared.

With nothing to do, my head went crazy, but I was no longer afraid of the craziness. I had often charted that familiar, uncomfortable, emotional seesaw in the pages of my journal. My verbal deprivation didn't change the nature of my craziness, just intensified it. I noted mentally that on the first day I'd covered a lot of ground during my walks, but hadn't seen much of anything. On day two, I did lots of walking and saw more, but not in great detail. By day three, I noticed a greater richness of colors, but the fresh air seemed to dull my mind. I couldn't remember what I was doing there — just that I had to stay for some unknown reason. The day was drizzly, foggy; I napped in between short walks.

On day four, I finally mellowed out and enjoyed the lack of routine — free from the demands of telephone and children and classes. I dawdled in the sunshine, strolled around, played with my bits of colored rock, driftwood, shell, and assorted flotsam — assembling a crude mosaic. I saw everything in minute detail, and enjoyed the varied hues and textures that fascinated me like the button box of my childhood. Until . . . I found myself feeling bored and discouraged again. I finally remembered that the main reason for taking this time out of my busy life was to find a new approach for my novel, but concentration was difficult; nothing productive was happening.

On the afternoon of the fifth day, I gave up and decided to go home the following morning, earlier than I'd planned. I felt more than a little foolish, once again a victim of unrealistic expectations. An hour later, I was sitting under a tree in the apple orchard listening to the intermittent chirping of baby birds. I could hear them clearly, but couldn't spot the nest. Warm sunshine bathed my face. A starling swooped away from a gnarled and twisted apple tree nearby; the leaves of the tree were greening, but no blossoms yet bloomed. The starling returned, her beak full; she perched near a cleft in the old tree, then dropped the worms. A loud and furious chirping ensued; she swooped away again.

Curious, I kept circling the tree, but still couldn't locate the nest. I drew back to watch more carefully. The mother bird, more cautious now, kept stopping to look my way. Then she darted in, dropped the food, and flew off again. I approached the tree, the starling scolding from a distance. I stood on tiptoe, the baby birds finally visible through a knothole. The center of the tree had a natural, protected hollow, hidden from below. I watched the fledglings hungrily searching, their scrawny necks stretching skyward. Their loud cheeping followed me as I backed off. The mother bird bawled me out, then resumed her pattern of feeding. I wandered around the orchard, bemused by the sight of the baby birds, struck by the fact that it had taken me five days to see something that was less than a hundred feet from my campsite.

Suddenly, in my mind's eye, I saw a woman moving through an apple orchard. It wasn't me; it was someone I'd never seen before. The woman's image was vivid in my mind; I could see through her eyes and knew what she was thinking; I knew her background and her life experiences. I knew the story she had to tell. And I knew that her story would use all the stuff from my life, all the adventures I'd wanted to use in a novel. But they would be somehow transmuted, so they would not really be mine; they would be subtly changed, and fully hers.

That scene was so rich, so deeply felt, that I needed no pencil, no paper. I knew I wouldn't forget it, never forget her. And I knew that there would be time to begin the writing of it. I was fascinated by the fact that only an hour earlier I'd given up thinking I'd find an idea for my book. Yet there I was, pregnant — with book. The idea and the character and the voice for the novel were different from anything I'd ever *thought up,* or tried to *think up.*

In some way, I'd let go, given up; and then, perhaps for the first time, I experienced that rich inner source of fiction I'd heard so many novelists speak of so glibly. I now had tangible evidence that I could actively collaborate with my subconscious. Now that I had identified what it felt like to experience the creative mode, I could consciously seek out and do those things that paved the way — the things that made it more likely to occur.

Many strategies can help you activate the creative mode. Try any of the following ideas that appeal to you to discover what technique works most effectively.

HOW TO ACTIVATE THE
CREATIVE MODE

- Precede writing time with thirty minutes or more of rhythmic, sustained exercise: walking, roving, running, swimming, biking, or any physical workout at home or elsewhere.

- Precede writing time with a relaxation process. Quieting the mind through meditation works wonders for some people.

- Play music during your writing session. Choose classical music or any mellow kind of nonvocal background music that will support your efforts without distracting you.

- Remove your wristwatch and keep clocks out of view. If you want to control the duration of your writing session, set a timer and place it out of sight.

- Write first drafts or zero drafts by hand. Or, if you're a good typist, try free flow writing in a darkened room. Shut your eyes while typing; cover or turn off the screen on your computer. No peeking; no going back to correct typos.

- Use a spiral notebook to begin each new project. Enter

thinking notes on the left-hand pages. Use the right-hand pages for your early draft what-if's and speculations.

- Before drifting off to sleep at night, visualize yourself sitting at your writing desk enjoying your writing sessions.
- Encourage yourself to write without thinking and write without stopping until your writing time is up, especially when you feel yourself slowing down or when you feel like stopping.
- Still feeling stuck? Try "smile meditation": sit down at your desk and smile. Don't think, just smile and see what comes to you. If nothing comes to you, give up thinking something different should be happening. Keep sitting there and keep smiling until you begin writing something. What you write is not important; the fact that you write is.

YOU KNOW YOU'RE IN THE CREATIVE MODE WHEN . . .

- You lose track of time, become absorbed in the doing. There's a sense of timelessness; you're totally caught up in the here and now of what's happening. No thought of past or future intrudes, and there's no concern for the outcome; there's just a oneness with the act of writing, the flow of words.
- Your consciousness of self disappears. If you're analyzing, trying to figure out if you're there yet, you're not.

It's only after the fact, when you emerge into the world again, that you realize you've been enjoying the creative mode.

- You feel totally accepting of the process and everything you're producing. Nondiscriminating, you do not judge, nor are you aware of distinctions such as right and wrong or good and bad.
- You feel pleasure, fun, delight, joy, satisfaction, and spontaneity. You catch yourself happily humming out loud.

Chapter Twenty-Two

Shaping to Form

Once you have generated a mass of raw material, the left brain takes over. That takeover, called rewriting, operates from the logical, critical mode. Beginning writers often hear that easy reading means hard writing. In truth, easy reading means lots of rewriting, taking the haphazard mass of raw material and shaping it to form.

Although content and idea are more important than form, form cannot be neglected if the material is intended for anyone else to read. Often writers will try to impose a more or less standard form upon their material, in an effort to *do it right*. The best approach to rewriting is an attitude of discovery, seeking to find the inherent form in each small section within the sprawling rough draft, and editing out or chipping away anything that does not serve the idea. Then comes the building-up phase when skeletal impressions are fleshed out and specific examples and more precise language are added.

Answering some essential questions before you begin rewriting can help you focus your rewrites.

WRITING EXERCISE #5
INTENTION AND AUDIENCE

This is best done as a self-interview, writing out the questions and answering them in a stream of consciousness flow of words on paper. The first series of questions can uncover your intention or purpose. Ask yourself:

What is my intention for writing this? Or rewriting this?

Why this particular story or subject?

What started me thinking about this idea?

Where did the notion of writing it begin for me?

Why is it important for me to write this?

Why am I the best person to tell this story?

Why now? Why is this the best time to write this?

Here's the final, and most important, question to consider; it concerns the potential reader of what you're writing. This question is crucial, especially if you're writing for a wider audience than yourself. Ask yourself:

Who am I writing this for?

Writers usually want as many readers as possible. Aiming for too wide an audience, however, can result in a fuzzy focus. The solution is to think of a specific individual, someone you know or have known personally, to stand in for that larger audience you desire. Then, when you rewrite, keep that person firmly in mind as you decide what to expand or what to leave out. Thinking about the reaction of this one person can help you make the myriad decisions that constitute the rewriting process. Caution: Do not show what you are writing to this person; his or her opinion will only confuse the issue.

This self-interview exercise evolved from class discussions about stories that felt unclear or off track. I would keep asking questions until the writer came up with the real reasons for writing that particular piece. Invariably, the answers provided information that belonged in the piece itself. Think of the rewrite process as a series of steps to be taken one at a time, rather than something that happens all at once. Break the job of rewriting down into specific tasks such as checking the logical flow of ideas or scenes, checking the accuracy of facts or character development, and checking for grammar, spelling, and punctuation problems.

I discovered that the process of rewriting was similar to the process of rock polishing. After my island vacation from words, a friend noticed that my box of beach rocks and pebbles (the ones I'd arranged and rearranged) looked dull and lusterless unless they were wet — then they came alive with color. That friend gave me a rock-grinding kit and I began polishing rocks just for fun.

Rock polishing has four major steps. The first is the rough, or coarse, grind; the chosen rocks are placed in a hard rubber barrel along with coarse metal filings and water; they tumble, nonstop, for ten days or more. The tumbling, grinding action mimics what happens at the beach, and the rough edges are eventually worn down. This stage is the longest of the four and, like the first stage of rewriting, it can't be hurried. Depending on how uneven the surface of the rock (or how crude the expression of the idea), this stage may need to be repeated to achieve the desired results. Some rocks don't polish well no matter how long they are tumbled; some ideas need to be discarded or abandoned, as well.

The second stage is the fine grind, a more refined grinding that clears away further imperfections and roughness. The rocks are rinsed and sorted, then returned to the barrel with fine metal filings to tumble for a week or more. Some rocks, especially those from ocean beaches, are so smooth to begin with that I can begin with the fine grind. Some writings are like that, too; not many, but some.

The third stage is the pre-polish, a shorter smoothing where the surface is readied for the polishing. The rocks tumble in a pumicelike slurry. Flaws often become visible during this stage and flawed rocks must either be returned to repeat an earlier stage or discarded. Similar treatment is necessary for any writing that does not come up to standard. The fourth and often final step is the polishing, where the rocks tumble in a solution of jeweler's rouge and water. In rewriting, this is where I go over the final draft, dictionary by my side, checking as I go.

Processing one batch of rocks can take three weeks or longer. When I've completed the final step of the process, I usually feel excited. With keen anticipation, I rinse off the red polishing compound and view the results: my pretty pebbles, my jewels. I delight in the colors and markings. As I check them over, I notice that some, though beautiful, are still flawed. Some look better than I'd suspected they might. Some are smooth, but not shiny like the rest, too soft to have anything but a matte finish.

My ideas and the rewriting process produce similar results — both surprises and disappointments. It took me several months to get the hang of choosing the best rocks to polish, and years to learn to choose the better ideas to work on. Eventually, I did get better at selecting those that show the most promise of ending up relatively unflawed. Unexpected problems, however, can arise. If the power goes off and stops the tumbler in midcycle, the resulting rocks are often uneven, lacking uniform luster. Occasionally they're unsalvageable. Likewise, if my writing gets interrupted for too long, I lose momentum, and sometimes lose the excitement I need for the first draft.

Each stage of rewriting has a different focus for me. My overriding concern, during the whole rewrite process, is clarity and good communication. Both of these reflect my respect for the potential reader, whether editor or friend. Each writing project has different demands, some more complex than others. Fiction seems to require more rewriting than nonfiction, for example.

In the final stage of rewriting, manuscript mechanics such

as spelling, punctuation, grammar, sentence structure, and paragraphing must be thoroughly addressed. Knowing how to spell accurately seems to be a genetic quirk; it has nothing to do with intelligence or higher education. Relying on a computer spelling-checker program seldom takes care of all problems, either. Therefore, if you're truly a poor speller, it's best to hire an intelligent typist for the final draft, a typist who will correct your typos and misspellings as part of the job. Punctuation is simply an aid to the reader, telling him or her when to pause, when to breathe, and what words or phrases to emphasize.

All the rules of both punctuation and grammar can be broken, or severely bent, *if* the result is clear and readable. The only criterion when writing for a wider audience is: *Does it work?* Does it work to clearly communicate what you want to the intended audience? In the case of fiction, does it evoke the emotional response you want from the reader? And, most important, is it satisfying for the reader?

Sometimes it takes a great deal of practice to feel comfortable and in command of both your creativity and your skills. It can be difficult to know when to collaborate with your subconscious, and when it's time to start shaping to form. As you become more familiar with your individual two-stage process you will be better able to accomplish your writing goals and dreams.

The following three-part Wordplay is designed to help you achieve understanding, cooperation, and synthesis between your creative and critical faculties. You can learn to operate your write-brain and make friends with your right- and left-brain personae. This exercise requires more time and energy than most of the others in this book. Plan on at least half an hour. A lighthearted, playful spirit is helpful, just as with all the other Wordplay exercises.

Hopefully, by this time you have a sense of the split between the two sides of you — the creative and the critical. Think up nicknames for them, as if each were a separate entity. Some names that students have used for the right-brain part of themselves are Creator, Child, Fun Lover, Daydreamer, Sweetie Baby. Often the diminutive of your given name works well; Jeanie, for instance, represents that creative playful part of me. Nicknames for the left brain include Critic, Teacher, Taskmaster, Watchdog, Quality Controller, Clyde.

WORDPLAY #12

1. Personify your left brain, using the projection technique. Call it by the nickname you've chosen. Think of it as a living entity. Enter into the playful spirit of this exercise; pretend you are the left brain, the part that loves to define and explain. Use the first-person point of view: "I am Taskmaster, Jean's critical self. . . ." Allow it to tell you about its education, its skills, its abilities, its preferences and prejudices, as well as its doubts and fears. Think of yourself as taking dictation.

Write without thinking. Write without stopping.
Begin now.

2. Repeat this process for the creative part of you. First name it, then become it on paper. Allow it to express itself fully. The right brain appreciates freedom and fun and movement; it tends to be unsophisticated in expression, and may use slang and childlike language. Let it tell you where it currently operates in your life, what it likes and dislikes. Use the first person: "I am Jeanie. I like to play with words."

Write without thinking. Write steadily.

Begin now.

3. After both sides have had a chance to fully express themselves, record a discussion between them on paper. Ask them to talk about how each of them can help you get your writing done. Let them work out together how each will contribute to actualizing your dreams of writing. Find out who will get you started and who will keep you going and how they will do those things. If either of them has fears or problems with the role of the other, now is the time for them to talk about it, to work it out, to come to some sort of agreement. Sometimes, at first, the best that can happen is that they agree to disagree.

You, the whole writer, can ask questions, but it's best to allow them to do most of the talking. Keep going with this until you feel a sense of completion, surprise, or satisfaction.

No thinking. No stopping.

Begin now.

If this doesn't work for you the first time, don't give up the idea. *Try at least three times.* Often, each writing experience using this format will be surprisingly different. Once you've established a reasonably friendly relationship with these two parts of you, it's possible to use them as a resource — to summon them up at will, and ask them for help or guidance with any writing difficulty.

This is something you must prove for yourself. I've never known it to fail when there's a willingness to try this Wordplay with an open mind. Problems arise when expectations are too high and when the spirit of playfulness is missing. Skepticism, on the other hand, can't hurt — if you explore that skepticism while doing the exercise, just for the fun of it.

Chapter Twenty-Three

Never Take Any Advice You Don't Agree With

If you've ever taken an English class, you've probably been advised to never end a sentence with a preposition. The title for this chapter and many sentences in this book end with a preposition. Does that make them wrong?

Advice is a tricky thing anyway. Most of us really don't want advice — especially during first-stage writing. We seek approval and appreciation; we want to share our excitement. Or, as English talk show host David Frost remarked, "What a writer means by constructive criticism is a few thousand words of closely reasoned adulation." Nevertheless, we eventually move into the rewriting stage, and then we writers do need or want useful feedback.

Beginning writers will often show their writing to friends or relatives and say, "What do you think?" Unfortunately, the responses can range from congratulatory to insulting. Both extremes can create confusion; neither produce comments that are useful. Unrealistic expectations can follow congratulations such as, "That's wonderful. Don't change a word. Send it out to get published immediately."

Too much encouragement or excessive praise can provide a momentary ego boost, but little you can use. Adverse reactions such as, "That's disgusting!" or "Surely you can do better than this" can be seriously discouraging, especially when the advice giver attacks your choice of subject, or proceeds to tell you in great detail how he or she would have handled the idea differently (i.e., their way). Too many *helpful* suggestions often feel like an invalidation of our ideas or ourselves. It's difficult not to take criticism personally, especially since we're personally involved with our choice of subject or story, and heavily invested in terms of time and energy.

Very few nonprofessionals will ask you what kind of feedback you want, or attempt to discover what you were trying to communicate, or even simply tell you what they gained from the reading. Participation in a compatible writers' group or class can help you discover what sorts of criticism you find most useful, and can train you to ask for the feedback you want.

When you solicit or accept reader response, you need to be involved with your writing, yet not overidentified with it. The paradox is that your stories and poems, your brain-children, need to be *intimately of you, but separate from you.* You need to cultivate a detached interest to effectively evaluate and use feedback, as well as filter out the possible bias of those who are giving you their advice. In other words, *consider the source* before you take any suggestions; understand that what people say about your writing often says more about them than it does about your work.

When it comes to advice, you need to trust your instincts. Otherwise, you try to take all the conflicting advice you're given, and your ideas get mangled or killed. If you always think others know more than you do about what you should be doing with your stories, your output and quality of writing can suffer. Writing is an act of faith in yourself and your vision. Works in progress are highly vulnerable, and it's important to pay attention to what nurtures your ideas and your writing habits so you can ask appropriately for what you really need.

You can also discover how to effectively communicate what you *don't* need. Cultivate enough ruthlessness to enable you to reject any comments that you don't understand or agree with — any advice that doesn't serve your writing.

Even the best-sounding advice is of no value at all if it's inappropriate, unappreciated, or misunderstood. You know you've received good advice when, after hearing it, you wish you'd thought of it yourself, or you have a spontaneous and genuine desire to try it out. One of my students, new to writing class, brought in the first chapter of a book and received conflicting suggestions for improvement. She returned to class the following week and announced, "I sorted the advice into three categories: suggestions I understood and agreed with and felt I could use; those I agreed with, but didn't know how to apply; and comments I either didn't understand or didn't agree with." Try this sorting process for yourself when you're feeling overwhelmed by criticism.

Everyone is a critic; each participant in a writing class or workshop has an opinion. However, it's likely that only a few people in any given group will have a sense of what you're trying to achieve with your writing. Therefore, you must learn to discriminate, to be ruthless in taking only advice that you agree with; this includes ignoring irrelevant or confusing feedback offered by the instructor or leader. The main problem with taking advice you don't agree with is that if you really don't agree with it, you are likely to subtly sabotage your best efforts; then, you lose trust in yourself and in the person who gave the advice as well.

All advice needs to be tentatively given; all suggestions taken with a grain of salt, if at all. In a group, listen respectfully to all criticism offered; never try to explain what you *really* meant. Never defend; never argue. If they didn't get it, it's your ultimate responsibility to clarify, but you do not have to take their suggestions. You decide which comments are valid and which are not. Learn to detach enough from what you've written to put negative criticism in perspective; it is possible to learn something from almost everyone. Anybody that discourages your belief in your writing or yourself, however, or anything that inhibits your production of the manuscript, is not constructive and should be avoided.

If you're serious about writing for publication, you can hire a professional evaluator to review your manuscript. Be prepared to ask for the kind of feedback you really want. Think about your expectations ahead of time; what you want to know.

Does my story work? Is it satisfying for the reader? Is it appropriate for the intended audience? What are its srengths? What are its weaknesses? What do I need to do to make it publishable? Can you give me specific suggestions for improvement? Questions such as these reflect a sense of apprenticeship, a willingness to revise under the guidance of a professional, and realistic expectations of what a successful manuscript evaluation can achieve.

Disappointment results from negative or vague questions such as: What's wrong with my writing? or, Do I have enough talent? Disillusion happens when you give your power away to the evaluator and neglect to be ruthless about not taking unhelpful advice, or if you expect a professional evaluation to ensure publication.

BEFORE YOU PAY THAT READING FEE

If you decide to pay for a professional critique, keep the following points in mind:

1. Do your homework. All critics are not equal, or interchangeable, or useful for you.

2. Evaluate your evaluator. Ask questions beforehand. Good rapport and mutual respect are essential. Ask for references if you have any doubts.

3. Understand the nature of the beast. Manuscript evaluation is not a science. At best, it's a helpful opinion based on experience and knowledge. There are no rules concerning writing for publication that haven't been broken (which does not mean that rules and guidelines are not valuable).

4. Know what you want. Do you want encouragement, or need help with ideas or story development? Do you want feedback on form, or content, or both? If you just want your grammar, spelling, and punctuation cleaned up, an intelligent typist might be a better choice than an editor. Do you prefer a written critique, or an in-person consultation? Sometimes the chance to ask questions can clarify the criticism. Tape recording the consultations can be very helpful.

5. Understand that you're in charge. You're the writer, the creator, the best expert on your own work. It's your byline that will appear on the published work.

Never take any advice that you don't agree with.

Chapter Twenty-Four

Can Anybody Get Published?

The question of whether anybody can get published deserves a book of its own. The short answer is *yes, if you want it badly enough to do whatever it takes*. There are some considerations about aiming to write for publication, however, that are helpful to be aware of while you're serving your apprenticeship.

The secret of getting published, it's often been said, is to have the right manuscript on the right desk at the right time. The writer can make sure that his or her written efforts are as well done and professionally presented as possible; the writer can also persist in keeping his or her manuscripts circulating, so that they are always on someone's desk (other than the writer's).

Besides these fundamentals, it's not enough that a piece of writing be both well written *and* interesting to get published nowadays. Your writing really has to have something more. That *something more* can be a matter of timing, transcendence, or both.

The timing of a book, however, is not that predictable.

From the time you begin writing to the final completion of the project can be a matter of months, or even years; so, timeliness alone is seldom the determinant of success. Something more is required. Transcendence is an elusive quality, hard to define, but a quality that most good editors recognize. So many editors say, "I know what I'm looking for when I see it in front of me." So much for asking an editor to tell you what he or she wants!

Transcendence arises out of personal conviction or passion, when the essential being of the writer is invested in the work. A clear intention and a sense of audience, coupled with a feeling of necessity that you, the writer, share this in written form, sets the stage for transcendence. This quality evolves from your interaction with the subject matter or story, and can seldom be planned or plotted lest it feel contrived for editors and readers alike.

Transcendence is a unique synergistic connection between the story and the writer, the kind of connection that results in the product being greater than the sum of its parts — you plus your writing creates a third entity — your brainchild. *The New Yorker* called transcendence "the third reality" in its "Talk of the Town" column:

> The characteristics that can create the third reality are, many of them, ineffable and unnameable. One that is instantly recognizable, however, and may even be a requirement, is care, without which

high quality is unattainable. Care is itself an artistic statement that expresses love. For example, a novelist who chooses compassion for his subject but then draws his characters sloppily really expresses contempt. On the other hand, a novelist who writes about underworld violence but takes the time and expends the energy to bring his characters, good and bad, into being, performs an act of love, a gratuitous act of caring, which stirs love in the reader as well and becomes the true statement — one could even say action — of the novel.

The ability to uncover the sanctity of every person, no matter how debased, and also to reveal the miraculousness, the preciousness of the humblest details of life is what makes the writing and reading of novels a humanistic enterprise of great importance: not just the creation and enjoyment of a diversion — though it can be just that — but acts to which one can appropriately bring one's most serious thoughts about life.

What are your most serious thoughts about life? If you had just six months to live, what would you write? What do you know to be true? Your subjects, themes, and stories need to be so special and important to you that no other person could write that piece in just that way. Your writings, fiction or nonfiction, must integrate your uniqueness with your stories or topics. If you are writing something that anyone else could write in the same way, let them do it. Choose those projects, or let them choose you, that have what one editor called "the thumbprint of the author."

Your books, ideas, and stories need to be personal as well as universal, a place where your experiences and your visions are honored. Your commitment to your ideas, your visions, needs to be intensely personal. When the value is in the doing, first and foremost, not just in the desire for an audience, then transcendence is more likely to occur.

Style may be part of what transcendence is about, since style simply is the writer. To write with style means to write truthfully — to write honestly, not to impress, but to express a conviction, to express your creativity, or just to entertain.

For the reader, the quality of transcendence manifests itself in evoking a response: an "Aha" when the reader experiences surprise, "Yes" when the feeling is profound satisfaction. That's the impact a good poem makes. James Dickey, novelist and poet, said that what he wanted in a poem was "a fever. A fever and a tranquility." Opposites; the juxtaposition and compatibility of opposites. Surprise! A sense of paradox, and a sense of acceptance and delight in that paradox. Here's the dictionary definition:

Transcendent: 1. going beyond ordinary limits; surpassing; exceeding.
2. superior or supreme.

Aim to go beyond ordinary limits with your writing. Remember that a laborer is someone who works with his hands, a craftsperson is someone who works with his hands and head, but an artist is someone who works with his hands, head, and heart. When you write, make sure all of your faculties are engaged: your hands, your head, and your heart.

Cultivate the following three attributes as you seek success in getting published: (1) persistence, which includes determination and hard work, (2) an open mind, which includes learning about yourself from your own struggles with words on paper, and (3) passion, which leads the way.

The struggle to write is always worth the time and effort. The dream of writing is always worth the cost. Write a lot; build up an inventory of articles and stories and books so you will be ready to take advantage of getting published when the time is right.

Begin now.

THE RISKS AND REWARDS OF A WRITING LIFE

1. Listen to your heart; writing from the heart offers the most satisfaction. The more you enjoy writing for its own sake, the more likely you are to achieve success with your writing.
You may have to change your idea of what success is.

2. If you wait until you're completely prepared, it will often be too late. Don't read too many books. Don't over-research. Don't wait until you think you know all the answers. Much has been accomplished simply because the writer didn't know it couldn't be done.
It is not possible to eliminate the risk of failure.

3. Follow your dream, if you're lucky enough to have one. Dreams transcend logic; it may not be possible to explain this to anyone.

4. Don't solicit opinions about your desire to write or get published. Your friends and relatives will give you their opinions anyway.
Do cultivate compassion for their concern, dismay, and occasional hostility regarding your choices.
Do not, however, be swayed by their fears, nor allow their unsolicited opinions to tarnish your dream.
Open-mindedness helps.

5. Your best interests are always served by respecting and serving your own needs, as well as those of your potential readers, and your editors — if possible.

6. It is not possible to write perfectly, nor even as well as you might like. Seldom will stories, or even nonfiction books, work out quite as you planned. Your success will be founded on writing despite these inadequacies.

7. A price must be paid for following your dream of being a writer. You will have no boss to blame for your daily writing difficulties, you will sacrifice much leisure time, and you must tell the truth and risk self-exposure.
The rewards of this writing life, however, are more often than not worth the risks.

Chapter Notes

Part One
Chapter Three

"covert curriculum of punctuality . . . rote-repetitive work."
— Alvin Toffler, *The Third Wave* (New York: Bantam Books, 1981).

"It is, in fact, nothing short of a miracle . . . a sense of duty."
— Albert Einstein, *Ideas & Opinions* (New York: Crown Publishers, 1954).

"To be a writer . . . give yourself away."
— Jessamyn West. Quoted in 1980 issue of *The Writer.*

"To write means to give all . . . risk we must take."
— Anaïs Nin, *The Diary of Anaïs Nin, Vol. 4—1944–1947* (New York: Swallow Press, 1969).

"Creativity . . . open to new things."
— Ronald Fieve, *Moodswing, The Third Revolution in Psychiatry* (New York: Morrow, 1975).

"The truly creative mind . . . alive unless he is creating."
— Pearl Buck. Quoted in *Press Women* trade journal in 1971.

Chapter Five

"I've not touched my book . . . but not a book."
— Sylvia Ashton-Warner, *Myself* (New York: Simon and Schuster, 1967).

"In my struggle to get my writing done . . . like any other work."
— Janet Frame, *The Envoy from Mirror City* (New York: George Braziller, 1985).

"quantity produces quality . . . struck by lightning."
— Ray Bradbury. Interview by Robert Jacobs, February 1976 issue of *Writer's Digest.*

Part Two
Chapter Six

"They who lack talent . . . Thus talent is a species of vigor."
— Eric Hoffer, *Reflections on the Human Condition* (New York: Harper & Row, 1973).

"Do it. That's what . . . much less lumpy later on."
— R. D. Culler, *Skiffs and Schooners* (Camden, Maine: International Marine Publishing Company, 1974).

Chapter Seven

"People will be most creative . . . and not by external pressures."
— Teresa Amabile. Interview by Alfie Kohn in September 1987 issue of *Psychology Today.*

"To be well known . . . What does it matter?"
— Gustav Flaubert. Quoted in 1972 issue of *The Writer.*

"If you are doing something you want . . . worry about the future."
— George Sheehan, M.D., *Running and Being* (New York: Warner Books, 1978).

Chapter Eight

"The murder of writing is reading . . . thought you had to say."
— Shana Alexander, *Talking Woman* (New York: Delacorte Press, 1976).

"The only good writing is intuitive writing . . . good stuff comes out."
— Ray Bradbury. Interview by Robert Jacobs in February 1976 issue of *Writer's Digest.*

Chapter Eleven

"Watch children at play . . . to be complete play."
— Madeleine L'Engle. Interview by Jean Caldwell in March 1982 issue of *Writer's Digest.*

Part Three
Chapter Thirteen

"There are some hours of agonizing doubt . . . almost of despair."
— Anthony Trollope, *Autobiography* (Out of print).

"I'm scared . . . darkness of my own mind."
— John Steinbeck, *Journal of a Novel: The East of Eden Letters* (New York: Viking Press, 1969).

"Every one of us gladly turns away . . . even indulge in speculations."
— Carl Jung, *Modern Man in Search of a Soul* (New York: Harcourt Brace Jovanovich, 1933).

"To know how to write is a great art . . . until you have the first."
— Jacques Barzun, *Beginning to Write* (Out of print).

"described experiences of being flooded . . . ideas, and diversions."
— Ronald Fieve, *Moodswing, The Third Revolution in Psychiatry* (New York: Morrow, 1975).

Chapter Fifteen

"I stay at my typewriter . . . I work very hard."
— Adela Rogers St. Johns. Interviewed in April 17, 1977 issue of *The Seattle Times* newspaper.

"Press on. . . . Persistence and determination alone are omnipotent."
— Calvin Coolidge, thirtieth President of the United States. Quoted in a MacDonald's (hamburgers) magazine advertisement.

"act as if it were impossible to fail."
— Dorothea Brande, *Wake Up and Live* (New York: Simon and Schuster, 1936).

"You are never given a wish . . . You may have to work for it, however."
— Richard Bach, *Illusions* (New York: Delacourt Press, 1977).

Chapter Sixteen

"I discovered my limitations . . . as well as my natural defects allowed."
— W. Somerset Maugham, *The Summing Up* (New York: Viking Penguin, 1972).

Chapter Seventeen

"There are men and books that teach . . . original writer in three days!"
— Rudolph Flesch, *How to Make Sense* (New York: Harper, 1954).

Chapter Eighteen

"I don't do housework. . . . I made my own cheese balls."
— Annie Dillard. Interview in *Harper's Magazine,* February 1974.

"Every person has his own natural . . . attempt peak accomplishment."
— Hans Selye, Ph.D., *The Stress of Life* (New York: McGraw-Hill, 1956).

Part Four
Chapter Twenty

"Writing comes very hard. . . . to live with the chaos of a first draft."
— Mark Harris, *Short Work of It: Selected Writing* (Pittsburgh: University of Pittsburgh Press, 1979).

"Cultivate in yourself a good similarity . . . universe surrounding you."
— D. T. Suzuki, *The Essentials of Zen Buddhism* (New York: Dutton, 1962).

"Boredom is not an end product . . . before the clear product emerges."
— F. Scott Fitzgerald, *On Writing* (New York: Scribner, 1985).

"Starting to write . . . After fifty pages the tedium wears off."
— Irving Wallace quote from 1979 issue of *The Writer.*

Chapter Twenty-One

"There is another kind of seeing . . . above all, an unscrupulous observer."
— Annie Dillard, *Pilgrim at Tinker Creek* (New York: Harper & Row, 1974).

Chapter Twenty-Four

"The characteristics that can create . . . most serious thoughts about life."
— Quote on "transcendence" from "Talk of the Town" column in the March 15, 1982 issue of *The New Yorker.*

Index

Index

WORKSHOP INFORMATION

For information about Roberta Jean Bryant's
workshops and manuscript evaluation services,
write, telephone, or e-mail her at:

Bryant Ideas
P. O. Box 31282
Seattle, WA 98103
(206) 324-4179
E-mail: bryantideas@hotmail.com

NEW WORLD LIBRARY
publishes books and cassettes that inspire and challenge
us to improve the quality of our lives and the world.

Our books and tapes are available
in bookstores everywhere.
For a catalog of our complete library
of fine books and tapes, contact:

New World Library
14 Pamaron Way
Novato, CA 94949

Phone: (415) 884-2100
Fax: (415) 884-2199
Or call toll free: (800) 972-6657
Catalog requests: Ext. 50
Ordering: Ext. 52

E-mail: escort@nwlib.com
Website: http://www.nwlib.com